Main Street Flavors COOKBOOK

K Hahn

Outskirts Press, Inc.
Denver, Colorado

The opinions expressed in this manuscript are solely the opinions of the author and do not represent the opinions or thoughts of the publisher. The author represents and warrants that s/he either owns or has the legal right to publish all material in this book.

Main Street Flavors
Flavors from Main Street America

V1.0

Outskirts Press, Inc.
http://www.outskirtspress.com

ISBN: 978-1-4327-1732-2

PRINTED IN THE UNITED STATES OF AMERICA

TABLE OF CONTENTS

Food Categories

Disclaimer: Main Street Flavors is comprised of recipes submitted by individuals who have contributed them. Some recipes are original, and some are derivations, or variations, on classic recipes or have been created & attributed to family or friends. The reader assumes all responsibility when using the recipes in this book, including any possible allergic reactions. Author & publisher do not guarantee the effectiveness or specific quality of any recipe within.

Main Street Merchants & Supporters *pages 103 - 201*

ꕥ ꕥ

- *Arcade Coffee & Sandwich Shoppe*
- *Chalet Suzanne®*
- *Rick DePalma - Realtor*
- *The Lake Wales Downtown Times*
- *The Gallery and Frame Shoppe*
- *Gary L. Bear Barber & Style Shop*
- *James R. Hahn Productions - Art Gallery*
- *Hidden Gardens Bed & Breakfast*
- *Mayer Jewelers*
- *MP Architectural Drafting & Residential Design*
- *The Mystic Moondragon*
- *Salon Salon*
- *Stuart Avenue Café*
- *Trés Jolie*
- *The Vanguard School*
- *Weaver & McClendon, PA*

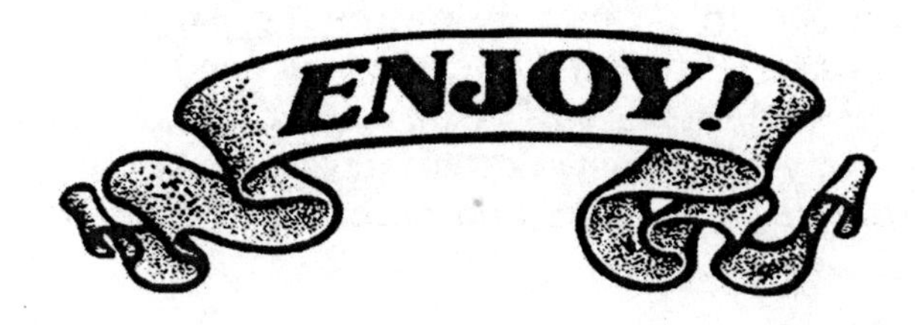
ENJOY!

Dedication

I come from a long line of strong and independent women. Some people have even described us as stubborn...very stubborn. This was the word, most often used, to describe my grandmother, Florence LaGrone.

She was a strong-willed, petite and beautiful woman, with a delightful, French sounding name. But to me... she was *Nanny*. I always assumed it was her real name.

Nanny lived with us, in our home, as part of our family. She and my mom were two, highly-opinionated women. They shared responsibilities and activities in the household, but it was Nanny who did all the cooking. And I mean...*all the cooking*. (This is where stubborn comes in.) She liked to cook, was good at it, and considered the kitchen her turf. She ruled the roost, called all the shots, made everything from scratch, never measured ingredients, never wrote any recipes down, and never told a soul how she made any of it.

It was sacred. It was private. It was *her* business. I've always heard the phrase, *"You can't take it with you when you're gone"*, but she did...She took it with her.

My sister, Jean, was born nine months before Nanny died. Her birth was truly a blessing for my parents. Mom was often heard telling family and friends, and I quote... "God took Mother and gave me Jean." She knew this to be true, we felt the same way.

My mother, having never really cooked, was now alone in an unfamiliar kitchen, with no family recipes to draw from, and no mentor to guide her. A reluctant cook was now in charge of Kitchen Patrol. Her inherited, *strong-will genes*, gave her the tenacity to persevere, figure things out, and find her way around the kitchen. We never missed a meal. Mom always managed to whip something up, which was fortunate, because my dad could not cook a thing. Not one thing. We teased him, unmercifully, by saying he couldn't fry an egg. He attempted this once... and his fried egg was scrambled. It was literally in pieces. We called this concoction *John's Scrambled Fried Egg!*

As Mom developed into a more seasoned cook, she would often reminisce about the times she stood next to her mother as they worked together preparing meals in the kitchen. These memories served her well. She retrieved treasured family recipes from the verge of extinction. Ironically, she followed her mother's example, and kept *these* recipes under lock and key. A few years ago, we successfully persuaded her to entrust these recipes to us for posterity. She presented us several index cards on which she had hand-written her favorite recipes. We treasure them. They are priceless. Some of her best loved recipes are included in this book and are being published for the first time.

My mother had quite a cookbook collection. They lined the shelves and tumbled out onto the floor. Recipes were crammed into every nook and cranny. I never quite understood why she had so many cookbooks...until now.

There is a fascination in scouting, researching and pouring over the personal details of what other people deem worthy of spending their valuable time and effort to prepare, serve and share with friends and family. Recipes speak volumes. Insight can be gained about one's personal tastes. Recipes are Rorschach Tests; ink blots where everyone who looks... will see something different.

I hope you enjoy this book... in many different ways

This book is dedicated, in loving memory, to my Mother...
Nell Lagrone Gheesling

Acknowledgments

In Appreciation

I would like to take this opportunity to express my sincere appreciation to all my many new friends in Downtown Lake Wales.

You welcomed us, with open arms, when we located our second art gallery in your beautiful Historic District. You made us feel as though we were a part of something very unique.

You have been very giving. You shared your own personal stories and family recipes. You supplied me a continuous flow of insights and anecdotes. And you have given me the love and support needed to write this book.

For that, I am very grateful... and honored to call you friends.

Thanks for filling the pages of this book with your own special blend of *Main Street Flavors*.

K Hahn

Foreword

The City of Lake Wales, Florida didn't get its moniker, "Crown Jewel of the Ridge", by random choice. It is a unique, big little city, with a special charm. If you stroll downtown just before the rising sun breaks the horizon you will be greeted with the heralding of a not too distant rooster.

The city is a familiar memory to many who have visited us, and even those who happened to read the Wall Street Journal years ago. On the front page, Lake Wales' own Spook Hill made its national debut on no less than a column and a half on the Journal's front page.

Spook Hill is a special place that defies gravity as cars roll backwards up a hill. It's part of our legacy, where an Indian chief saved an Indian village by killing a giant alligator that lived in the adjacent lake. The chief's spirit still expresses itself by defying gravity on the hill.

The downtown atmosphere still harbors the New Orleans flavor in subtle aromas of well-known *Vinton's New Orleans Restaurant*, which once stood on Stuart Avenue. A few nostalgic residents say if you pass by the old location at night, you can still get a hint of the spices used in their jambalaya. The owners of this restaurant once sponsored a culinary school. Many of the recipes that were once a part of our past, have filtered down to local residents and are now included in K Hahn's *Main Street Flavors.*

Chalet Suzanne is another restaurant that is so famous that diners have driven or flown in from remote cities to dine. The restaurant even has its own airstrip and is located less than five miles from downtown Lake Wales. Many of our fine restaurants have cultivated and influenced the taste of local appetites and are being featured in Hahn's cookbook.

As editor of the Lake Wales News, I have been blessed with the opportunity to be a part of Historic Downtown Lake Wales. I know you will enjoy this premier edition of K Hahn's ... *Main Street Flavors.*

H. Palmer Wood

Introduction

It was my intention to make ***Main Street Flavors*** a multi-faceted book. Within these pages you will find: an Art book, a History and Geography book, a Biography and to some extent, an Auto-Biography. For the day-tripper... ***Main Street Flavors*** is a Day Planner and Travel Guide. And last, but not least ... Drum roll please ... ***Main Street Flavors*** is a Cookbook. It is a celebration of life; shared with good friends, who enjoy good food.

My husband and I opened our art gallery, *James R. Hahn Productions*, in downtown Lake Wales after visiting the area and falling under the spell of the Historic Rhodesbilt Arcade. This castle-like building, listed on the National Registry of Historic places, now houses our art gallery and working studio.

Our local Main Street reflects a diverse mix of International culture. We are all dramatically different; but our love of food, and passion for eating, unite us. We form a sundry cast-of-characters with a continuous flow of diverse acts. These acts are seamlessly intertwined ... making for one very interesting play. Picture yourself on a walking tour of downtown Lake Wales. Imagine strolling along the sidewalk, and winding your way into interesting shops and galleries. The aroma of freshly brewed coffee from a sidewalk café will draw you inside. Peruse a menu and sample tasty cuisine from the many fine downtown eateries.

A cookbook that reflects Main Street America, with its unique sense of community, seemed like a good idea. Apparently, there were many others of you who felt the same way. This book is the first in a series of cookbooks featuring historic, Main Street America. It is a collection of community recipes, including insights and anecdotes from individuals, families, and hometown merchants who are proud to support and promote their own Historic Downtown. The Historic District is a quintessential destination that will appeal to your taste buds...and pull at your heart strings.

My fascination with Historic Downtown, and the amazing characters who weave in and out of it, was the inspiration for this book. - K Hahn

About the Artist

The cover of this book was created by the artist
James R. Hahn.

To Jim ... my multi-talented husband, artist and true Renaissance Man. This book would not have been possible without your love and support. Without your skill and talent, my book would have a blank cover, and my life would be shades of gray.

You paint my world beautiful...everyday.

Polk County is the Real Deal...

Located in sunny, central Florida, Polk County lives up to its name as the Lake District as it is home to 554 sparkling lakes. With an abundance of nature preserves, slow rolling hills, and warm and sunny climate, Polk County exudes a natural warmth and charm that is authentic Florida.

The area is steeped in history, teeming with rich aromatic citrus groves, and because of its convenient location, you are only minutes away from major attractions, world-famous theme parks, national parks, water sports, and top rated golf courses.

For a unique shopping experience, go downtown to the Historic District where streets are lined with quaint boutiques, art galleries, antique shops, gift and jewelry stores. Local merchants offer a wide variety of things you will not find in chain stores or area malls. The storefronts are not of the cookie-cutter, modular or pre-fab variety. These buildings are unique and appealing works of architectural genius and are listed on The National Registry of Historic Places.

Nestled among Downtown's colorful shops and galleries, are numerous restaurants, pubs, sandwich shops and cozy cafes serving some of the most mouth-watering foods, brewing fresh steaming coffees and blending healthy, all-natural fruit smoothies you will find hard to resist.

You can go to a large and impersonal chain restaurant in almost every city you visit. However, dining in the Historic District is so much more than just eating out. It's more than just satisfying your hunger...it's about feeding your soul.
Take your time and immerse yourself in the rich history and culture that is Lake Wales, FL.

A special monthly event in Lake Wales is ***Friday Night Live*** on the 3rd Friday of each month. Between the hours of 6-9 pm., Main

Street literally comes alive with a downtown street festival. Many of the downtown merchants stay open late to participate in this monthly, family event. Listen to live music being performed from various stages throughout downtown. Ride a horse-drawn carriage on a tour of this historic city. Wild animal exhibits featuring white tigers and exotic birds are always a hit with kids of all ages.

Check out the cute and cuddly dogs and cats the ***Polk County Humane Society*** brings to this event. These animals really steal the show. Of course these wonderful pets are looking for a home and are ready for adoption.

Bike Night roared into downtown Lake Wales last year and has met with great success. On the second Saturday of each month, bikers converge downtown where they mix and mingle with other bikers, enjoy live music and street venders and show off their *"rides"*. Check out the bike show where plaques are awarded for winners of the following categories.: American Cruiser - Antique - Custom - Ladies Class - Sportster - Sports Bike and Trikes.

Mardi Gras is celebrated in February with day-long festivities, ending with a spectacular parade, featuring a large assortment of unique floats. Revelers gather downtown along the parade route to catch the treasured Mardi Gras beads that are thrown to the crowds, by the handfuls, during this colorful celebration.

The annual ***Christmas Parade*** in December is a fun place to come for family Holiday fun in downtown Lake Wales.

Art lovers come from all across the nation to admire the outdoor murals that are located throughout the Historic District. The latest creation was painted by ***James R. Hahn Productions*** and is on Stuart Avenue, across from the Rhodesbilt Arcade. This 80-ft, tropical gardens mural was commissioned by ***Lake Wales Murals & Enhancements, Inc, and Salon Salon.***

From Historic Downtown, you can branch out like spokes on a wheel, to nearby destinations.

For beach lovers, either coast is only an hour-and-a-half away. Where else can you watch the sun rise over the Atlantic Ocean and see a spectacular sunset over the Gulf of Mexico? Now, that is one fabulous day trip. Put this on your *Life List* of Things to Do.

The list of fun activities in Polk County is almost endless. Modern adrenaline junkies can live on the edge in contrast to peace-seeking nature lovers who want to feel as though they just stepped back in time. There is something here for everyone. Polk County offers a diverse mix of both man-made and natural wonders.

For a more in-depth exposé on Polk county, refer to the back of the book, after the recipes ...

Appetizers

Orange Cream Cheese Dip

Ralph Morrow

1 package cream cheese, softened
1 carton orange yogurt (or vanilla)
½ cup orange marmalade
¼ cup finely chopped pecans

In bowl, blend cream cheese until smooth.
Fold in remaining ingredients.
Chill.

Serve with: Sliced apples or other assorted fruit.

Florida Orange and Sour Cream Dip

R. J. Reed

1 can (6-oz) frozen orange juice
1 package instant vanilla pudding
¼ cup sour cream
1 cup milk

In bowl: combine thawed orange juice, vanilla pudding mix and milk.
Blend with wire whisk until smooth.
Stir in sour cream.
Cover and chill for 2 hours.

Serve with: Assorted fresh fruit.
Arrange fruit on serving tray for guests to enjoy.

Note - This is a great party dip and a little out of the ordinary.

<u>Main Street Nachos</u>

The Downtown Gang

1 lb ground beef
½ cup onions
¼ cup green peppers
1 pint taco sauce
1 can refried beans
1 can cream of mushroom soup
1 envelope dry taco seasoning mix
Salt and pepper to taste

Toppings:
2 cups shredded cheese
Tortilla chips
Lettuce
Chopped tomatoes
Sour cream
Guacamole

Brown beef, onions and peppers, drain.
Combine all ingredients (except toppings)
Cover and cook on High for 1 hour. (slow-cooker)
Or simmer on stovetop for 15-20 minutes.

To Serve: Arrange Tortilla chips onto a large serving platter. Ladle the beef mixture over the chips, spoon on some sour cream, and layer all the remaining toppings.

You can serve the beef mixture in a separate bowl and arrange the toppings, in smaller bowls, around it. This way, your guests can scoop up just the toppings they want.

Chalet Suzanne®
Restaurant and Inn

Chalet Suzanne's Broiled Grapefruit

1 Grapefruit, at room temperature
3 Tablespoons Butter
1 teaspoon sugar
4 tablespoons cinnamon-sugar mixture
(1 part cinnamon to 4 parts sugar)

Slice grapefruit in half and cut membrane around center of fruit.

Cut around each section half, close to membrane, so that the fruit is completely loosened from its shell.

Fill the center of each half with 1½ Tbsp. butter.

Sprinkle ½ tsp. sugar over each half, then sprinkle each with 2 Tbsp. cinnamon-sugar mixture.

Place grapefruit on shallow baking pan and broil just long enough to brown tops and heat to bubbling hot.
Remove from oven and serve hot.

A grilled chicken liver placed on the center of each grapefruit provides the final flourish.

Makes 2 servings.

For over 75 years, Broiled Grapefruit with Grilled Chicken liver has been the featured appetizer, the first course of Chalet Suzanne's six-course Candlelight Dinner. The Grilled Chicken Liver was not part of the original dish, circumstances were the mother of invention. In the 1950's, at a dinner hosted by a national food processor and attended by Clementine Paddleford, New York Herald Tribune food editor, the Grilled Chicken Livers were not ready in time to be served as an hors d'oeuvre; but they were ready by the time the first course, Broiled Grapefruit, was to be served. Vita Hinshaw, at the last minute, garnished each grapefruit serving with a Grilled Chicken Liver and a new tradition was begun.

Located four miles north of Lake Wales, Florida, the Chalet Suzanne Restaurant and Inn has been welcoming guests for a meal or a night since 1931.

Cajun Stuffed Mushrooms

Linda Bell Pineda
Salon Salon

24-ounces Mushrooms
5 tablespoons butter
1 chopped onion
1 stalk finely chopped celery
4 slices bread (made into crumbs)
1 clove garlic, minced
1 tablespoon dried parsley flakes
½ teaspoon salt
Dash cayenne pepper
Grated Parmesan cheese

Remove stems from mushrooms and chop.
Melt butter and sauté onion, celery, and garlic.
Add stems and cook a minute longer.
Add parsley, salt, pepper, and cayenne.
Mix in bread crumbs. Stir well.

Stuff mixture into mushroom caps.
Roll caps into Parmesan cheese.

Arrange mushrooms onto a baking sheet.

Bake @ 350° F. for 20 minutes.

Note - These stuffed mushrooms taste great.

Layered Taco Dip
Erica Clark

1 can (16-oz) refried beans
½ cup taco sauce
¾ cup sharp cheddar cheese
1 package cream cheese, softened
¼ cup sour cream
3 tablespoons mayonnaise
¼ teaspoon garlic powder
1 large avocado, chopped
1 medium onion, chopped
1 tablespoon lemon juice
1 tomato, seeded and chopped
½ cup sliced black olives
½ cup sliced green onions

Stir together refried beans and taco sauce.
Spread evenly in bottom of 2-quart glass dish.
Spread half of cheese over beans.
In small bowl, combine cream cheese, sour cream,
mayo and garlic powder. Beat until smooth.
Spread over cheese.
Blend avocado, onion and lemon juice in blender or
mixer until smooth. Spread over cream cheese.
Sprinkle chopped tomatoes, olives, green onions, and remaining
cheddar cheese.
Chill up to 4 hours.

Serves: 10

Served with taco chips, this dip makes a great snack for a Super
Bowl Party or during a Florida State football game.

Maddox Street Salmon Patties
Nell Gheesling

1 tall can Salmon
1 cup fine bread crumbs
1 diced onion
2 eggs, beaten
Dash of Parsley
2 teaspoons lemon juice
Salt and pepper to taste
Mix salmon with bread crumbs.
Add eggs.
Fry in oil until brown.*
Remove from pan and drain patties on paper towel.

**Note - I use a butter-flavored cooking spray instead of the oil my mom used when she made these salmon patties.*
This will reduce both fat and calories, making a delicious and nutritious meal, high in heart-healthy omega oil.

Baked Salmon Muffins
Gene Bennett

1 can salmon
2/3 cup milk
1 cup bread crumbs or saltine crackers
1 tablespoon lemon juice
1 egg, slightly beaten
Salt and pepper to taste
Mix together all ingredients.
Pour into muffin tin.

Bake @ 350° F. for 1 hour.

Note - This baked salmon makes an unusual presentation served as a muffin.

Serve with: Green Salad and sliced fruit at a luncheon or light brunch.

T's Party Meatballs
Arcade Coffee & Sandwich Shoppe
Curt and Terry Koch

3 lbs lean ground beef
1½ cups plain/or seasoned bread crumbs
½ cups finely chopped onions
2 teaspoons roasted garlic (optional)
¾ cup milk
3 eggs
2 teaspoons parsley flakes
2 teaspoons salt
¼ teaspoon pepper
2 teaspoons Worcestershire sauce
1 large jar Grape Jelly (20-32 oz)
2 (12-oz) bottles Chili Sauce (Heinz)
1 (18-oz) bottle Honey Barbeque Sauce
Non-stick cooking spray

Mix ground round, bread crumbs, onion, garlic, milk, eggs, and seasonings.
Shape into 1-inch balls.
Spray large griddle or very large frying pan with non-stick cooking spray.
Brown meatballs. Remove from skillet and drain fat.
Heat chili sauce, grape jelly, and barbeque sauce in skillet until jelly is melted.

Transfer sauce to crock-pot and add meatballs.
Heat on High for at least 1 hour. Reduce to Low heat.

Terry sometimes prepares the meatballs the day before an event and refrigerates them until she and Curt are ready to party. Make sure to allow more warming time in crock pot.

Substitute: Little smoky links for meatballs.
Serves: Lots.
Serve with: Miller Lite

Terry's Tasty Chili Dip
Arcade Coffee & Sandwich Shoppe
Curt and Terry Koch

2 cans Hormel chili/no beans
1 (8-ounce) package Cream Cheese
1 cup sour cream
½ cup shredded cheddar cheese
Tostido Scoops or Frito Scoops
Chopped onion (optional)

In saucepan over medium/low heat,
melt cream cheese and sour cream.
Add 2 cans of chili, shredded cheese
and chopped onion, if desired.
Heat until bubbly.
Place in small crock pot to keep warm.
Serve with Tostido or Frito Scoops.
Great served with... BEER

Note - Curt and Terry invited "the gang" over one evening after closing, and Terry whipped up this dip in just a few minutes. This chili dip was the first food I had eaten all day long and it was really good. Terry was right... it is great with beer.

Onion Quiche

Dorothy Kenney

4 onions, thinly sliced
1 tablespoon olive oil
3 tablespoons butter
3 eggs
1 cup half-and-half
2 tablespoons flour
¼ teaspoon nutmeg
2 teaspoons salt
1/8 teaspoon pepper
2 ounces grated Swiss cheese

Prepare and partially cook a pie crust.

Sauté onion in olive oil and butter until soft and yellow.
Beat together eggs, cream, flour, salt, pepper, and
¼ teaspoon nutmeg, with half the Swiss cheese.
Place onions in pie crust.
Pour egg mixture over the onions.
Sprinkle the remaining cheese over the top.

Bake @ 375° F. for 25-30 minutes.

Serves: 6
Serve with: Any kind of roast.

Note - Dorothy uses a store-bought pie crust to save time making this quiche.

Chicken Pizza Pitas

R. Cope

4 pita rounds
1/3 cup Ranch salad dressing
1 (90-oz) package frozen chicken breast strips
½ cup diced onions
½ cup diced bell peppers
½ cup shredded cheese
Hot sauce to taste

Pre-heat oven to 450° F.

Place pita rounds onto pizza pan.
Coat pitas with Ranch dressing.
Arrange chicken strips, onions, and peppers on top of dressing.
Sprinkle cheese on top of pitas.

Bake uncovered for 12-15 minutes, or until pitas are heated through and are crisp and brown.

Great for appetizers or party snacks.
These are fast and easy to make and are bursting with flavor.

Note - Add additional Ranch dressing and/or hot sauce as needed to taste.

Substitute: Southwestern flavored chicken strips to give this recipe an added kick.

Breads

Nell's Holiday Dressing
Nell Gheesling

Start with one pan of cornbread:

Use an entire 2 lb-bag of yellow cornmeal
Add ½ cup self-rising flour
3 eggs
1 tablespoon salt
Add water until mixed well - not too thin

Note- My mother used a very large and heavy, cast iron skillet.
She cooked her cornbread in oil, on the stove top.
This is the authentic way to prepare this. My mother learned this recipe from my grandmother, and they both cooked it this way.
You can also *bake* this cornbread, cooking until golden brown.
Set aside and cool.
When cool enough to handle, crumble cornbread into small pieces and put into a large bowl.

Next step is the bread mixture
This will be added to the cornbread mix from step 1

1½ large loaves of white bread, crumbled fine
Sauté 5 onions and 6 pieces of celery (finely diced)
Add to bread mixture
Mix in 1½ sleeves of saltines
Add 5 eggs
Add turkey broth until smooth, but not too thick
Add *"a couple of shakes"* of poultry seasoning
Add seasoned salt and pepper to taste

This mixture will be very thick. Mix well. Bake @ 350° F. for 50 minutes, or until dressing is golden brown.

Serving size: A very large, family-sized pan.
Cut sections into serving size squares after dressing has cooled slightly.
Any leftover dressing heats up beautifully, and even tastes better as the flavors blend.

Substitute: Canned chicken broth, or even fat-free chicken broth for a healthier alternative.

Author's note - This is the first time this recipe has been shared with anyone outside of our immediate family. My mother was as reticent about her recipes as she was about her private life.

In the dressing recipe, you will note that the poultry seasoning amount is for, and I quote, "a couple of shakes". This was the official amount required in this family recipe, and was as specific as you could ever get this guarded cook to be.

I must tell you...one of my most vivid childhood memories is the intoxicating aroma of this holiday dressing, wafting out of my mother's kitchen. Enjoy!

Now that *Nell's Holiday Dressing* has been officially published, I hope you will share it with your family.

Thanks, Mom!

Nell's Biscuit Muffins

Nell Gheesling

2 cups self-rising flour
¼ cup mayo
1 cup milk

Mix well and pour into muffin tin.
Bake @ 350° F. for 18-20 minutes.

These are simple and quick and turn out great every time.

Serve with: Soups, Stews, and Salads.

French Onion Biscuits

Jake LaSalle

2 cups Biscuit Mix
¼ cup milk
1 container French Onion Dip

Mix all ingredients together until soft dough forms.
Drop onto greased baking sheet.

Bake @ 375° F for approximately 10 minutes.

Serve with: A thick French Onion soup combined with a tossed green salad.

Note - Also good with a variety of Chicken Stews and Vegetable Casseroles.

Cinna-Magic Sweet Potato Biscuits
C. R. Branch

1 large (16-oz) can Sweet Potatoes, drained
2 tablespoons cinnamon sugar
¼ cup milk
1½ cups Biscuit Mix

In mixing bowl, mash sweet potatoes.
Add cinnamon sugar and milk.
Beat until creamy. Stir in Biscuit Mix.
With fork, mix until most lumps are gone.
Knead dough 5-6 times on floured waxed paper.
Press dough to a thickness of about ½ inch.
Cut biscuits out of dough using a cutter or small glass.

Use spray butter (optional) to coat top of biscuits.
Sprinkle Cinnamon Sugar on top of biscuits.

Bake @ 375° F. for approximately 12 minutes or until biscuits are done.

Olive Loaf
Sid Burke

1½ cup Biscuit Mix
½ cup chopped ham (optional)
½ cup sliced green olives
1 egg, lightly beaten
4 tablespoons olive oil
¼ cup dry white wine
½ cup Swiss or Gruyere cheese

Pre-heat oven to 400° F.
Coat a 5½ x 3 x 2-inch loaf pan with cooking spray and lightly dust with biscuit mix.
Chop ham and olives in food processor until finely chopped.
Place 1½ cup Biscuit Mix, egg, Olive oil and wine in bowl.
Fold in ham, olives and cheese.
Divide batter evenly among 3 prepared loaf pans or muffin tins.

Bake for 22-25 minutes or until golden brown.

Run sharp knife around edge of pan to loosen loaves.
Serve hot with olive oil for dipping Italian style.

Serve with: Caesar salad, or try a fresh green salad with Balsamic Vinaigrette dressing.

Note - You can freeze loafs for up to 3 months.
Make extra loaves to simply heat and serve when unexpected guests pop in.

3 Ingredient Muffins
R.J. Reed

2 cups Biscuit Mix
1 stick melted butter
1 cup reduced-fat sour cream

Pre-heat oven to 350° F.

Combine Biscuit Mix, butter and sour cream.
Spoon mixture into ungreased muffin tin.
(Filling each tin only 2/3 full)

Bake for 15-18 minutes or until muffins are golden brown.
Servings: Approximately 2 dozen small muffins.

Note - These muffins are extremely easy to make, tastes great, and turn a gorgeous, golden brown color when baked.

Florida Orange Zest Corn Cakes

R. J. Reed

2 Florida oranges
1 package Jiffy yellow cake mix
1 package Jiffy corn muffin mix
2 eggs
1/3 cup milk

Pre-heat oven to 375° F.

Mist 2 muffin tins with cooking spray to eliminate sticking.
Rinse oranges and use a grater to create one tablespoon orange zest.
Juice oranges and set aside ½ cup of juice.

Combine cake mix with 1 of the eggs and ½ cup of orange juice until well combined.
Mix cornbread mix and remaining egg.
Add cornbread batter and orange zest to cake mixture, blend.
Spoon into muffin tins to 2/3 full.
Bake both tins, side by side in oven for 15-20 minutes or until golden brown.

Servings: Approximately 15-18 muffins.

Note - Using half cornbread mix and half cake mix is the secret to the sweet, cake-like texture of these muffins. Substitute orange juice (from a carton) if you do not have fresh oranges. Fill any empty muffin cups with water before baking to keep muffin tin from burning or warping during the baking process.

Mexican Cornbread
Rufus M.

2 packages cornbread mix
2 large eggs
1½ cups buttermilk
1 can green chilies, undrained
1 cup Mexican cheese

Pre-heat oven to 450° F.

Combine cornbread mix, eggs, milk,
Chilies (with liquid) and cheese.
Mix just enough to combine and moisten.

Bake for 18-20 minutes or until cornbread
is golden brown.

*Note - Use a 9-inch square or round pan
that has been lightly coated with cooking spray.*

Served with: a hot bowl of your favorite soup or with a hardy black-bean chili.

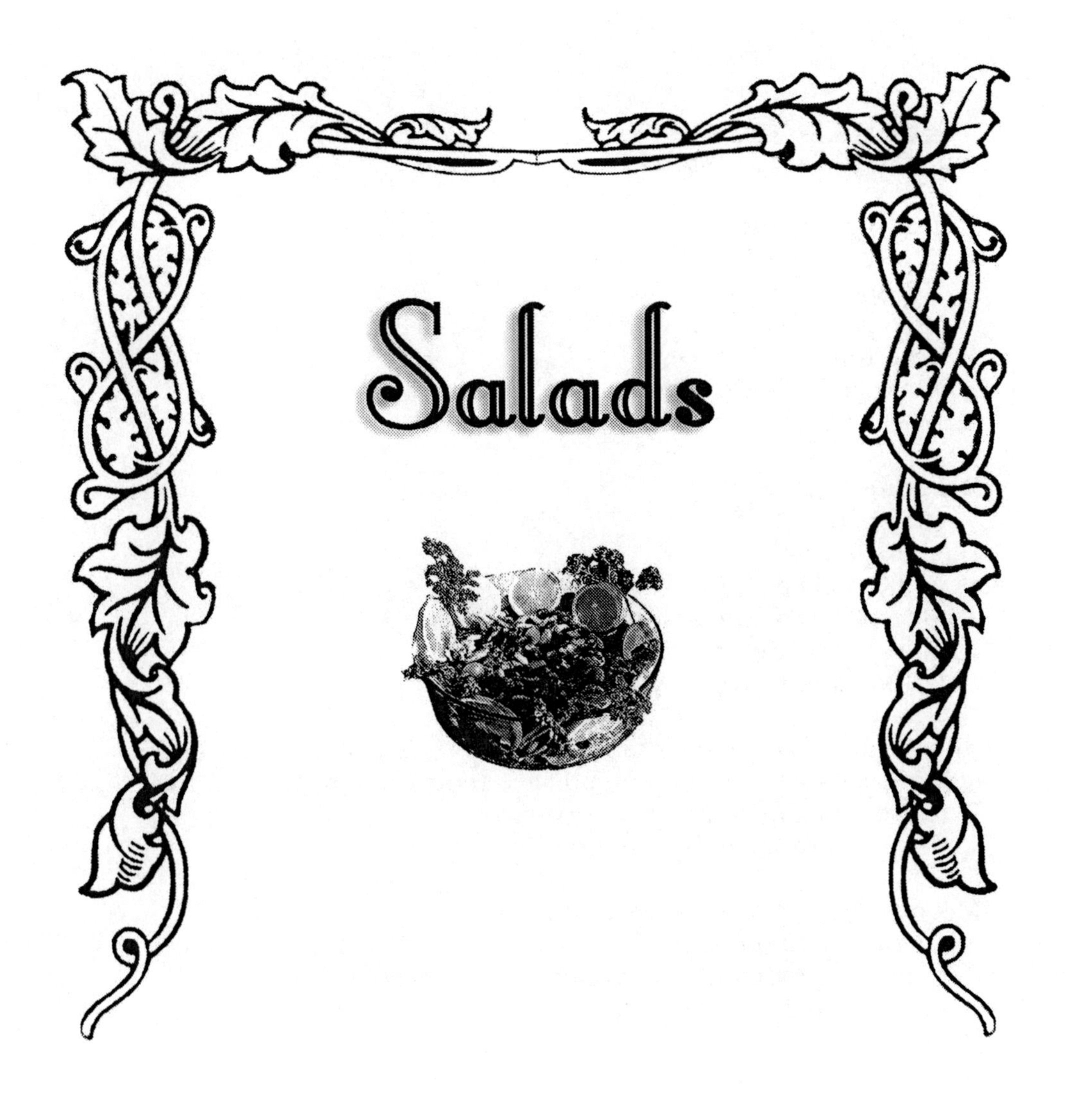

Salads

Mandarin Salad

Scott and Tammi Carter

Salad Ingredients:

½ cup sliced almonds
3 tablespoons sugar
½ head iceberg lettuce
½ head romaine lettuce
2 whole green onions, chopped
1 (11-oz) can mandarin oranges, drained

Dressing Ingredients:

½ teaspoon salt
Dash of pepper
¼ cup Canola oil
1 tablespoon chopped parsley
2 tablespoons sugar
2 tablespoons Tarragon Vinegar

In a small saucepan over medium heat, cook almonds and sugar, stirring constantly until almonds are coated and sugar is dissolved.
Watch carefully, as this will burn easily.
Cool and store in air-tight container.

Mix all dressing ingredients and chill.
Mix lettuce and onions.
Just before serving, add almonds and oranges.
Toss with the dressing.

Serves: 6

This Mandarin Salad is very refreshing.
It is the perfect dish on a hot, Florida afternoon.

Broccoli Salad

Beverly Simpson

Salad Ingredients:

2 bunches fresh broccoli
½ cup raisins
1 medium onion or onion powder
12 slices bacon
1 cup shredded cheese
1 cup peanuts

Dressing:

1 cup Miracle Whip
½ cup sugar
2 tablespoons vinegar

Mix all ingredients. (except cheese)
Allow to stand 2 hours in refrigerator.

Before serving, toss salad.
Add 1 cup shredded cheese.
Serve and enjoy.

Serves: 6
Serve with: Soup and a crusty French bread.
Also good with assorted wheat crackers, and sliced fruit.

Note - The peanuts add to the crunchy and refreshing appeal of this Broccoli Salad.

Hot Chicken Salad

Kitty Moseley

4 cups cooked chicken, diced
2 tablespoons lemon juice
¾ cup mayonnaise
1 teaspoon salt
2 cups chopped celery
4 hard-boiled eggs, diced
1½ cups crushed potato chips
¾ cup condensed cream of chicken soup
1 teaspoon minced onion
2/3 cup finely chopped roasted almonds
1 cup grated cheese

Combine all ingredients, except almonds, cheese and chips.
Place in greased casserole.
Top with almonds, cheese and chips.

Let stand overnight in the refrigerator.

Bake @ 400° F. for approximately 30-35 minutes.

Serves 8

Note - This is my husband's Aunt Kitty. She lives in Jacksonville, Florida.

Hot Fruit Salad

Dot Hahn

1 can fruit cocktail, reserve juice
2 cups sliced tart apples
1 cup dark, sweet cherries, halved
(or canned dark cherries, drained)
1 can sliced peaches, drained
1 can pineapple chunks, drained
1 cup dried plums, pitted and halved
Slivered almonds

Layer the above 7 ingredients in a 9 x13 inch baking dish.
Arrange slivered almonds on top.
Spoon sauce (recipe below) over fruit.
Bake @ 350° F. for 1 hour, uncovered.

Sauce:
1 cup light brown sugar
2 teaspoons curry powder
1 stick margarine
2 teaspoons cinnamon
3 tablespoons cornstarch
2 teaspoons nutmeg
¼ teaspoon salt
Juice reserved from fruit cocktail

Melt margarine in pan.
Add sugar, cornstarch, spices, salt and juice.
Spoon over fruit.

Note - This is a great source for your daily serving of fruit. This luscious salad can also be served as a dessert with whipped cream or, if you're really daring... a scoop of ice cream.

Blueberry Congealed Salad
Dot Hahn

2 packages of sugar free raspberry Jello
1 can blueberries, drain/reserve
1 small can crushed pineapples, drain/reserve

Dissolve the Jello in 3 cups boiling water.
Add blueberries, pineapple and 1 cup of the 2 juices to the Jello and mix well.

Put into a 9 x 13 inch baking dish that has been lightly coated with cooking spray.
Refrigerate to congeal.

Topping:

1 (8-ounce) package cream cheese
1 cup sour cream
1 teaspoon vanilla
4-5 packs of Sweet & Low
1 cup crushed pecan pieces

Combine cream cheese, sour cream, vanilla and sweetener.
(substitute ½ cup of sugar if desired.)
Mix well and spread over congealed salad.
Sprinkle crushed pecans over top.

Note - This is a family favorite. It is gone in a flash.

Congealed Cranberry Salad

Dot Hahn

2 packages cranberry Jello
(substitute lemon Jello if cranberry is unavailable)
1 can whole cranberry sauce
1 small can crushed pineapple, undrained
2-3 packs Sweet & Low

Use 3 cups boiling water to melt Jello.
Mix well.
Add the cranberry sauce.
Blend in the crushed pineapple and Sweet & Low.
Mix well.

Pour into a 9 x 13 inch dish that has been lightly coated with cooking spray. Refrigerate salad to congeal.
(You can make this salad the day before if you like.)

Topping:

1 8-ounce package cream cheese
1 cup sour cream
1 teaspoon vanilla
3-4 packs Sweet & Low
1 cup pecan pieces (use more to taste)

Mix together cream cheese, sour cream, vanilla & Sweetener.
Spread mixture over top of congealed salad.
Sprinkle pecan pieces on top.

Note - This is a different approach to the traditional Cranberry sauce that is typically served at Thanksgiving.
Try this colorful and festive treat during the Holidays...
You will get Rave Reviews.

Potato Salad by Ted

Dorothy Kenney

2 lbs new potatoes, cooked, cooled and diced
2 hard-cooked eggs, chopped
1 cup chopped, seedless cucumbers
¼ cup chopped onion
¼ cup chopped green pepper
¼ cup vinegar
¼ cup water
2 tablespoons sugar
1 tablespoon mustard
1 cup mayo (for dressing)

Beat the two chopped, hard-cooked eggs.
In saucepan, bring vinegar, sugar, mustard and water to a boil.
Add a small amount of this hot mixture to eggs.
Blend and then add to boiling mixture.
Cook over medium heat, stirring for 5 minutes, or until thickened.

Place chopped vegetables in salad bowl.
Mix 1 cup of mayo with the hot mixture.
Pour over the chopped vegetables.
Toss to blend.

Serves 6
Serve with: Barbeque

Note - This is a two-man recipe. Dorothy's husband chops the vegetables while she cooks the dressing. Great teamwork.

Wilted Lettuce
Rev. Marilyn Spry

Head of lettuce
1 medium/large onion
2-3 slices of bacon
1 egg
¼ cup each: water, vinegar, and sugar

Wash, dry, and tear lettuce into pieces.
Slice onion and separate rings.
Place lettuce/onion pieces into bowl, set aside.

In skillet, fry bacon until crisp.
(Drain off grease, leaving some for flavoring in pan.)
Beat egg and mix well with water, vinegar, and sugar.
Pour mixture back into pan with bacon.
Cook until thick, stirring continuously.

Pour mixture over lettuce and serve immediately.

Serves 4-6

Great served with: *ANYTHING*

Note - This is a Spry family favorite.
It is so good that you can make it an entire meal.
Marilyn says this is especially good with leaf lettuce.

Layered Lettuce Salad
Ron Ericson

1 head of lettuce, cut into bite size pieces
1 cup of diced celery
4 sliced hard-boiled eggs
1 (10-oz) package frozen peas (do not thaw)
½ cup diced bell pepper
1 medium onion, sliced
8 slices of bacon (fried crisp and crumbled)
2 cups of salad dressing
¼ lb shredded cheddar cheese

Arrange in order all ingredients (except cheese)
in 9x13-inch pan.
Sprinkle cheese over salad.
Cover with plastic wrap or pan lid.
Refrigerate overnight.

Serves: 9-12
Serve with: Hot Rolls

Note - You can substitute any other vegetable for peas, but Ron has found peas to be very tasty.

You can make a light and healthy meal of just the salad.

Nell's Watergate Salad

Jean Ufret

1 container Cool Whip
1 box pistachio instant pudding
1 cup chopped nuts
1 cup mini-marshmallows
1 small can crushed pineapple
Shredded coconut, to taste

In large bowl, mix all ingredients together.
Blend well.
Chill in refrigerator, until ready to serve.

Great served as a dessert, after Sunday dinner.
Leftovers can be stored in the refrigerator.

Author's note - My mom made this salad quite often. As the name implies, this salad was made famous at the Watergate Hotel. It is light, sweet and fruity. This salad is easy to make, and only takes a few minutes to whip together. It is especially good in the spring and summer, as it is cool and refreshing.

<u>Frozen Cranberry Salad</u>

Ellen Saliba

2 (3-oz) packages cream cheese (softened)
2 Tablespoons mayonnaise
2 Tablespoons sugar
1 can *whole* cranberry sauce
1 small can crushed pineapple
1 cup chopped pecans
1 cup whipped cream (or you may use Cool Whip)

Combine softened cream cheese, mayo and sugar.
Blend well.
Stir in cranberry sauce, crushed pineapple (undrained), and pecans.
Fold in whipped cream.
Place in oblong Pyrex dish and freeze.
Take out 10-15 minutes prior to serving.

Author's Note - Ellen is my sister-in-law and lives in Birmingham, Alabama. This recipe is special to Ellen. It originally came from Shauna Saliba many years ago. Frozen Cranberry Salad is a holiday tradition in the Saliba home.

Ellen serves this dish every Thanksgiving and Christmas. Her family won't let her forget it, ha!

7 Cup Fruit Salad
K Hahn

1 cup mini-marshmallows
1 cup fruit cocktail
1 cup crushed pineapple
1 cup sour cream
1 cup coconut
1 cup nuts
1 cup mandarin oranges

Mix all ingredients together.
Chill for 8 hours

This salad is very simple to make and easy to remember.

7 cups / 7 ingredients = 7 Cup Salad.
Love the math -- Even a Blonde can do it.

Vegetables

Maddox Street Squash Casserole

Nell Gheesling

2 lbs fresh squash (cooked or canned) drained
½ stick of butter
2 eggs
½ cup onions
1 cup crushed saltine crackers
1 cup milk
Salt and pepper to taste
Buttered bread crumbs

Add butter, onions, cracker crumbs and eggs to fresh cooked squash. (Or use canned.)
Mix well.
Add milk and mix.
Pour into buttered dish and top with bread crumbs.
Bake @ 350 F. for 30 minutes.

Note - My mom made this squash for our family; and we still make it this way. It is so good... it makes me hungry just to think about it.

Maddox Street Scalloped Corn

Nell Gheesling

1 lb. can cream-style corn
1 egg
1 cup crushed saltine crackers
2 tablespoons butter
2 tablespoons chopped onion
Salt and pepper to taste.
Combine all ingredients, mix until blended.
Bake @ 375 F. for 30 minutes.

Cheese Hash-Browns
Ron Ericson

1 stick butter
½ lb Velveeta cheese, cup up
1 (8-ounce) carton sour cream
1 can chicken soup, undiluted
1 small chopped onion
1 (2-lb) bag frozen Hash Browns
Bread crumbs (for topping)

Melt the butter in a saucepan.
Add the cheese and stir over medium heat,
until the cheese is almost melted.
Remove from heat. Add sour cream, soup and onion.
Mix well. Add Hash browns and mix well.

Pour mixture into a buttered 9x13-inch baking dish.
Lightly sprinkle top of potato mixture with bread crumbs.

Bake @ 350° F. for 30 minutes.
Serves:10
Serve with: Toast and Eggs

Note - Ron likes to take this dish to a Pot Luck dinner.

Spinach Pecan Vegetarian Pie

Brandy Johnson

4 cups chopped fresh spinach
2 tablespoons butter
½ cup chopped bell pepper
1 cup chopped onion
3 large eggs
1½ cups grated cheese (Swiss or Cheddar)
1¼ cups half-and-half
½ cup chopped pecans
Salt and pepper to taste
1 (9-inch) pre-baked pie shell

Sauté onions and peppers in butter, until tender.
Add chopped spinach and continue to sauté until wilted.

In pre-baked pie shell: arrange chopped pecans and grated cheese on bottom.
Spread the wilted spinach mixture over cheese layer.
In separate bowl: blend eggs, half-and-half, salt and pepper.

Pour mixture into pie shell, covering cheese and pecans.

Bake @ 350° for approximately 30-35 minutes, or until a knife inserted into center of pie comes out clean.

Note - This is Brandy's favorite vegetarian recipe. It was a hand-written treasure that she received from a family friend.

She says that every time it is served, she gets rave reviews.

Broccoli Whiz Casserole

Brandy Johnson

1 jar Cheese Whiz
1 package frozen broccoli, cooked
1 can mushroom soup
1 cup cooked rice

Lightly mist casserole dish with cooking spay.
In bowl, mix together the cooked broccoli, cooked rice, jar of Cheese Whiz and the mushroom soup.
Pour into prepared casserole dish.

Bake @ 350° for 30 minutes, or until bubbly.

Note -This recipe is easy to prepare. Experiment by adding leftovers such as ham or turkey to the basic recipe. Brandy takes this dish along when she is asked to bring something to a party or family get-together.

Serve with: Hard rolls, slathered in butter.

Vegetable Bake Casserole

Sandy Smithe

1 can asparagus
1 can green beans
1 can English peas
1 can cream of mushroom soup
1 can water chestnuts
1 can sliced mushrooms
½ lb sharp cheddar cheese, grated
½ cup dry bread crumbs
Salt and pepper to taste

Lightly mist casserole dish with cooking spray.
Drain canned vegetables and arrange in layers in dish.
Slice water chestnuts and layer over top.
Pour mushroom soup over vegetables.
Place sliced mushrooms over top of mixture.
Scatter grated cheese over all.
Top with buttered bread crumbs.

Bake @ 350° for 40 minutes.

Note: Sandy likes using canned vegetables for their convenience, but suggests that you can also use fresh vegetables for this recipe. Cooking time may vary.

This is a great vegetarian recipe as it includes several different vegetables. Take this meatless dish to a covered dish event and you will be a hit with any vegetarian there.

<u>Parmesan Zucchini</u>
Sandy Smithe

1½ - 2 lbs whole zucchini
½ cup grated Parmesan cheese
½ cup dry bread crumbs
¼ cup butter, melted
Salt and pepper to taste

In boiling, salted water, parboil whole zucchini for 10-12 minutes, until tender.
Remove pot from stovetop and drain water.
Split zucchini in half lengthwise and place on broiler pan.
In small bowl, combine cheese, bread crumbs, salt, pepper and butter.
Spread mixture on top of sliced zucchini.

Place pan under broiler for a few minutes until cheese is melted and bread crumbs are browned.

Note - This fast and easy vegetarian dish has a rich, hearty flavor. Serve this as a delightfully different hors d'oeuvres.

Serve with: Excellent side-dish for any number of main dish entrees. Great served with fresh sliced tomatoes.

Fry Daddy Squash Puppies
Sandy Smithe

5-6 medium fresh squash, sliced
1 beaten egg
½ cup milk or buttermilk
1 medium onion, finely chopped
¾ cup self-rising cornmeal
¼ cup flour
Salt and pepper to taste

On stovetop, cook squash in boiling water, over medium heat, for approximately 15 minutes, until squash is tender. Drain.
Mash squash with fork. Combine with remaining ingredients.
Drop batter, by tablespoons, into Fry Daddy for 5 minutes or until squash puppies turn a golden brown.

Servings: 2-3 dozen puppies, depending on size

Note - (Hot oil @ 350°) when cooking in a deep-fat fryer or in a heavy skillet on stovetop. Oil needs to be very hot for quick cooking.

Option: Add a small can of corn (drained) to the batter for a variation that tastes more like corn fritters.
Sandy especially likes to add Mexi-Corn when she makes this recipe, as the red peppers give the Squash Puppies a dash of color.

Spinach & Black Bean Lasagna

John Howard

2 cans black beans, rinsed and drained
1 jar pasta sauce
½ teaspoon ground cumin
1 container ricotta cheese
1 pack frozen spinach, thawed and drained
2 eggs slightly beaten
9 (no boil) lasagna noodles
1 package Monterey Jack cheese w/jalapenos

Pre-heat oven to 375° F.

Place beans in bowl and mash until smooth.
Stir in pasta sauce and cumin. Set aside.
In separate bowl, mix ricotta cheese, spinach and eggs.
Spoon 1/3 of the bean mixture over bottom of 13 x 9-inch baking dish. Arrange 3 of the noodles side by side lengthwise on top of beans.
Spoon ½ of spinach mixture on top and spread.
Scatter 1 cup of cheese over. Arrange 3 more noodles.
Add beans and last 3 noodles. Top with beans.

Cover with foil and Bake 40-45 minutes.
Remove foil and top with rest of cheese.
Re-cover dish with foil and let sit 10 minutes.
Cheese will set up and lasagna will be easier to cut.

Italian Spinach Pie Casserole

Elizabeth Ezekiel

1 lb cottage cheese
3 unbeaten eggs
¼ cup American cheese, cut up
¼ cup margarine, cut up
1 package, frozen chopped spinach (cooked/drained)
3 tablespoons flour
Salt to taste

In bowl, combine cottage cheese, eggs, American cheese, cooked spinach and flour.

Pour mixture into a greased pie plate.
Bake @ 350° F for 1 hour or until pie is set, and crust is golden.

Serves: 8-10

Note - This is a rich and tasty addition to any meal. Italian Spinach Pie Casserole may be served hot or cold. This casserole re-heats well in microwave.

Copper Pennies

Dot Hahn

2 lbs carrots
1 cup sugar (or 12 packs Sweet & Low)
½ cup oil
1 teaspoon Worcestershire sauce
Salt and pepper to taste
1 can tomato soup
¾ cup vinegar
1 teaspoon prepared mustard
1 medium bell pepper, finely chopped

Scrape carrots, slice and boil until tender. Drain.
Mix remaining ingredients well. Pour mixture over cooked carrots.

Cover and refrigerate overnight.

Note - Every time Dot serves this ... everyone loves it.
This dish is great with a side salad and served with your favorite entrée.

Swiss Vegetarian Bake

1 large bag frozen Vegetables, thawed
(broccoli, cauliflower, carrot mix)
1 can cream of mushroom soup

1/3 cup sour cream
½ cup shredded Swiss cheese
1 can French Fried Onions
Black pepper and salt to taste

Stir together mushroom soup, sour cream,
thawed vegetables, salt, pepper, 2/3 cup of Fried Onions
and ¼ cup of Swiss cheese.
Pour into a 2-quart, buttered casserole dish.

Cover and Bake @ 350° F. for 45 minutes.

Remove casserole from oven and stir to mix.
Sprinkle remaining Swiss Cheese and French
Fried onions over top of vegetable mixture.

Bake for an additional 5 minutes or until cheese has slightly
melted.

Serves: 4
Serve with: Hot baked cornbread or biscuits.

Entrées

Tuna Spud Cakes

R. Cope

1 cup refrigerated mashed potatoes w/garlic
1 can tuna, drained and flaked
1/3 cup fine cracker crumbs (Saltines/Ritz)
¼ cup minced onion
2 tablespoons vegetable oil
Salt and pepper to taste

Combine potatoes, tuna, cracker crumbs, salt and pepper.
In skillet, heat oil over medium heat.
Drop 1/3 cup of potato mixture into hot oil.
Flatten with fork to about ½ inch thick.

Cook until golden brown, approximately 5 minutes.
Gently turn with spatula and brown other side.

Drain on paper towel.

Serve with: Tartar sauce or lemon juice.

Great with a green salad or fruit salad.

Chicken Bake Ole
Donna James

2 cups cooked chicken, cup up
1 can tomatoes with chilies
½ cup chopped onions
½ teaspoon ground cumin
1 cup sour cream
1 cup Monterey jack shredded cheese
¾ cup shredded cheddar cheese
1 egg
Salt and pepper to taste
2½ cups corn chips

In mixing bowl, combine chicken, tomatoes, onion, cumin, salt and pepper. Mix well and set aside.
In separate bowl, blend sour cream, ¾ cup cheddar cheese, Monterey Jack and egg.
Spray dish with cooking spray.
Spread half of corn chips in casserole. Layer ½ chicken mixture and half of sour cream. Repeat layers.
Top with remaining corn chips and ¼ cup of cheddar.

Bake @ 350° F. for approximately 1 hour or until chicken is done and golden brown.

Note - Pre-cook chicken a few minutes in microwave to insure doneness and shorten cooking time.
On the Grill: Pre-heat grill for 10 minutes.
Grease 2-quart grill-safe casserole. Arrange layers as above.
Bake over Medium heat, with hood closed, until chicken is done and heated through.

Chicken Martini

C. Moon

1½ lb boneless chicken breasts
5-6 tablespoons butter
¼ lb fresh sliced mushrooms
1½ cup white wine
1 can artichoke hearts, quartered
1 clove garlic, minced
Salt and Black Pepper

Sauté chicken in butter until done and
no longer pink inside.
Add minced garlic and white wine.

Simmer on low for 15-20 minutes.

Add mushroom and artichoke pieces.
Salt and pepper to taste.
Stir to blend and heat thoroughly.

Serve with: Rice or pasta and a side of green beans.

Chicken Jambalaya Stir-Fry

Chuck Patten

8 boneless, chicken thighs, cut up
2½ cups Vegetable juice cocktail
1 16-ounce bag frozen stir-fry pepper mix
½ cup diced cooked ham
1 tablespoon vegetable oil
¼ teaspoon garlic salt
1 teaspoon hot sauce
¼ teaspoon pepper
1¾ cups quick-cooking rice, uncooked

Sprinkle garlic salt and pepper onto chicken pieces.
In large skillet, heat oil over medium heat.
Arrange chicken and cook until lightly browned.
Add vegetable juice, ham, pepper stir-fry mix, and hot sauce.
Heat to boiling, reduce heat, cover and simmer on low for 5 minutes.

Stir in rice and heat to boiling.
Cover and remove pan from heat.

Let stand 5 minutes or until rice and vegetables are tender and liquid is absorbed.

Lobster & Crab Casserole

C. Moon

½ lb lobster meat
½ lb crab meat
1 large finely chopped onion
¼ cup finely minced celery
1 can diced tomatoes with peppers, drained
1 can mushroom soup, undiluted
1 cup evaporated milk
½ cup almond slivers
¼ cup chopped pimento
1 can asparagus tips, drained
½ lb crushed Ritz crackers

Sauté onion and celery in butter.
Add diced tomatoes and cook until tender.
Turn off heat and allow to cool several minutes.
Add mushroom soup, milk, almonds, and blend well.

In buttered casserole, sprinkle ½ of the Ritz crackers in bottom of dish and add the following in layers:
Asparagus tips, 1/3 mushroom soup, ½ lb lobster meat, 1/3 mushroom soup, ½ lb crab meat and remaining mushroom soup. Layer remainder of crackers over top.

Bake @ 325° F. for 30 minutes.
Serving option: Sprinkle a little cheddar cheese on top during the last 5 minutes of cooking.
Serve with: Wheat Rolls or Croissants.

Note - For Entertaining ... you can make it ahead of time and just pop the casserole in the oven when guests arrive.

Beef and Pepper Grilling Kabobs
Chuck Patten

1 lb beef sirloin steak-cut into bite size pieces
2 medium bell peppers (one red-one green for color)
1 medium onion, cut into wedges
8 cherry tomatoes
1 (8-ounce) can tomato sauce
½ cup orange juice
1 tablespoon Worcestershire sauce
Salt and pepper to taste

Combine tomato sauce, orange juice and Worcestershire sauce in bowl and mix together to make marinade. Set aside.

Place cut up steak pieces in bowl with marinade and mix well to coat each piece of beef. Cover and marinate in refrigerator for 2 hours or up to 24 hours in advance.

Remove beef from bowl - reserve marinade. Alternately thread beef, peppers and onions onto 8 long, metal skewers.

Place kabobs directly onto grill, over medium heat.
Grill for approximately 15 minutes, turning occasionally and brushing with reserved marinade.
Cook until beef is done.

Place cherry tomato onto the end of each kabob and return to grill for just a minute or two longer, until heated through.

Oven Broiled Variation:
Broil kabob in oven for approximately 15 minutes, turning and brushing with marinade, until beef is done. Place cherry tomato onto end of kabob and return to oven to broil another few minutes until tomato is heated through.
Serves 4

Meatball Casserole

John Simms

1 package frozen meatballs, cooked
2 cups cooked, mixed vegetables
1 16-ounce can diced tomatoes
1 tablespoon vegetable oil
½ cup onion
½ cup green pepper
1 clove garlic, minced
2 tablespoons all-purpose flour
1 teaspoon sugar
¼ teaspoon dried basil
1 teaspoon beef bouillon granules
1 tablespoon Worcestershire sauce
1 can refrigerated buttermilk biscuits
Salt and pepper to taste

Preheat oven to 400° F. Heat oil in pan and sauté onion, garlic and green pepper until tender.
Stir in sugar, basil, salt and pepper.
Blend in tomatoes, vegetables, meatballs, Worcestershire sauce and bouillon granules.
Cook until mixture thickens and is hot and bubbly.
Pour into a 2-quart casserole dish.
Place unrolled biscuits on top of casserole.

Bake uncovered for approximately 15 minutes, or until biscuits are golden brown.

Makes about 4 servings.

Gourmet Party Chicken

Rev. Marilyn W. Spry

8 boned, skinned chicken breasts
8 slices thin bacon
1 package chipped beef
1 can undiluted mushroom soup
½ pint sour cream
2 tablespoons dry sherry
Garlic powder

Dust chicken breasts lightly with garlic powder.
Wrap each chicken breast with one slice of bacon.
Mist baking dish with cooking spray.
Cover the bottom of the baking dish with chipped beef.
Arrange chicken breasts on top of beef.
Mix together the soup, sour cream*, and sherry.
Pour mixture over top of chicken.

Bake @ 275° F. for three hours, uncovered.

Serves: 6-8

Serve with: Wild Rice, Green Peas and a Salad.
Best when cooked slow at low temperature.

*Rev. Spry uses fat-free sour cream in her recipe.

Note - Rev. Spry is a retired minister with 42 years of service, who enjoys entertaining. Marilyn likes this recipe because it is quick with little, last minute preparation, so she can spend time with her guests.

Marilyn's Ham Loaf
Rev. Marilyn Spry

½ lb fresh ground pork
1 lb ground ham
(a good butcher will grind them together)
1 cup Saltine cracker crumbs
2 eggs
1 cup tomato juice
¼ cup brown sugar
Garlic powder, onion powder, and pepper to taste

Mix all ingredients thoroughly.
Form mixture into a loaf and place in pan.

Bake @ 350° F. for 1½ hours.

The last half hour, cover with ½ cup of tomato juice.

Serves: 8

Serve with: Baked Sweet Potatoes and a Salad.

Note - Marilyn often prepares this dish when she has company, and her Ham Loaf has been featured at Easter time.
Her guests find it very tasty and enjoy it with Horseradish sauce.

Baked Spaghetti

Marty Haney

1 cup chopped onion
1 cup chopped green pepper
1 tablespoon butter or margarine
1 can (28-oz) diced tomatoes, undrained
1 can (4-oz) mushroom stems and pieces, drained
1 can (2½ oz) sliced ripe olives, drained
2 teaspoons dried oregano
1 lb ground beef, browned and drained (Optional)
1 lb spaghetti, cooked and drained
2 cups (8-oz) shredded cheddar cheese
1 can (10-oz) condensed cream of mushroom soup, undiluted
¼ cup water
¼ cup grated Parmesan cheese

In large skillet, sauté onion and green pepper in butter, until tender. Add tomatoes, mushrooms, olives, and oregano.
Add ground beef, if desired.
Simmer, uncovered for 10 minutes.
Place half of the spaghetti in a greased 13x9x2-inch baking dish.
Top with half the vegetable mixture.
Sprinkle with 1 cup of cheddar cheese. Repeat layers.
Mix the soup and water until smooth. Pour over casserole.
Sprinkle with Parmesan cheese.

Bake uncovered @ 350° F. for 30-35 minutes or until heated through.

This is a favorite dish for the Haney family get-togethers.

Note that the ground beef is optional. Omit this step for a meatless baked spaghetti.

Fran's No-Peek Chicken
Fran Wills

1½-2 lbs chicken breasts, legs and wings
3 cans cream of celery soup
3 cans cream of mushroom soup
6 cups milk
1 box minute rice (7-8 cups)
2 cans water (use soup cans)
3 packages, dry, onion soup mix
Salt and pepper to taste
Spice as desired

Pre-heat oven to 350° F.

Line bottom of large roaster with aluminum foil, leaving foil long enough to fold back over the entire chicken. Seal well for easier clean up later.
In large bowl, mix together soups, milk, and uncooked rice.
Add any other seasonings at this time, as desired.
Pour mixture into roaster, smoothing with spoon.
Arrange chicken pieces on top of rice mixture.
Sprinkle dry, onion soup over chicken.
Fold aluminum foil up and over chicken.

Cover *Airtight.* Bake @ 350° F. for 2 hours.

Do not lift lid, do not peek, don't even think about looking inside that roaster until 2 hours are up. (This insures chicken is properly cooked.)

Note - For quicker bake time: precook chicken, and the entire meal will cook in approximately 40 minutes.

Serves: 8

Additional serving Suggestions/Substitutes

For added versatility, add any combination of the following:

½ cup chopped celery, leeks, onions, broccoli
¼ cup chopped green onions, mixed green/red peppers
Garlic, sage, thyme, and pepper to taste.
Chopped leftover turkey, chicken, or ham

Line bottom of roaster with refrigerator biscuits or
Roll out biscuits to lay on top, or both, ala pot pie.

Substitute any other soup flavor for different taste.

Grate cheddar cheese and melt over top during the last
10-15 minutes of baking.

Note - A tossed green salad is a good compliment to this dish. Also, try an assortment of fresh fruit, or sliced tomatoes. Arrange fruit on a decorative platter for a healthy balance to this delicious meal.

Ultimate Beef Brisket

Anna Crutcher

Ingredients:
7 lbs beef brisket
1 teaspoon garlic salt
1 teaspoon onion salt
1½ teaspoon salt
1½ teaspoon pepper
1½ teaspoon celery salt
2 tablespoons Worcestershire sauce

Sauce:
½ cup granulated sugar
1 cup barbeque sauce
1 cup broth (from cooked brisket)
1 cup Russian Dressing (not creamy)

Mix seasonings and Worcestershire sauce together.
Rub sauce into meat.
Wrap tightly in heavy-duty aluminum foil.
Place meat in a 9x13-inch baking pan, or roaster.

Bake @ 275° F. for approximately 7-8 hours.

Remove pan from oven. Remove foil covering.
(Reserve 1 cup of broth for sauce.)
Discard all remaining broth. Trim brisket of any excess fat.
Cut meat into slices and return to pan.
Mix together all ingredients for sauce.
Pour sauce over brisket slices.

Bake @ 300° F. for 1 hour.
Serves: 6

Mama DePalma's Coq au Vin

Rick DePalma

1½ - 2 lbs Chicken breasts, cut up
2 cans cream of Mushroom soup, undiluted
¾ cup dry, white wine
Sliced Swiss cheese
Salt and pepper to taste
Croutons

Arrange chicken pieces into a baking dish.
In separate bowl, mix cream of mushroom soup together with white wine.
Pour mixture over chicken.
Season to taste.
Cover with sliced, Swiss cheese.
Sprinkle with croutons.

Optional: Pour melted butter over croutons

Cover dish with aluminum foil and Bake @ 350° F. for approximately 1-1½ hours.

Uncover, and Bake for an additional 10-15 minutes, or until croutons are golden brown.

Serve with: Caesar salad and hot Italian or Garlic bread.

Note - Rick got this recipe from his mother, Angie DePalma. This is one of his all-time favorites.

Corn Chowder

Linda Bell Pineda
Salon Salon

4 tablespoons butter
1 lb sliced Kielbasa or imitation crab meat
1 medium chopped onion
2 cans chicken broth
1 cup instant mashed potatoes
½ cup milk
2 (10-oz) packages frozen corn

Melt butter.
Add sliced Kielbasa. Cook until browned.
Add chopped onions. Cook until browned.
Turn down heat. Add all remaining ingredients.
Let stand for a few minutes before serving.

Serve with: Corn bread. Yum!

Substitute: Crab meat for Seafood Corn Chowder.

Note - This is the favorite dish of Linda's son, Abe.

Creole Steak
Lisa Pederson
The Gallery and Frame Shop

1 lb cube steak
Oil for frying
1 large can stewed tomatoes
2 bell peppers
2 onions
Salt and pepper to taste
Flour

Dredge steak in salt, pepper and flour.
In hot oil (grease to those from the South) brown steak until coating is crisp. Meat does not have to be done.
Remove from oil, drain and set aside.

In same pan, pour off all but a tablespoon or two of grease.
Leave all the "crispies'" in the pan.
Add one large can of stewed tomatoes, "squished" of all juice.
Cut onions and bell peppers into rings.
Add peppers and onions to tomatoes.
Bring to a boil and reduce heat.
Add fried steak and cover.

Simmer for 30 minutes.
Simmering will finish cooking the steak and also tenderize it.

Serve with: Over rice, as a side to the steak.

Note - This is a classic, Southern dish that Lisa's mother taught her to make. The Creole Steak recipe was passed down from Lisa's grandmother. No one knows how far back this recipe goes.

Scalloped Salmon

Lisa Pederson
The Gallery and Frame Shop

1 can pink salmon, (drained, skinned and boned)
2 tablespoon butter/margarine
1 egg
2 tablespoons flour
1 cup milk
Saltine crackers

Place salmon in mixing bowl. Flake. Set aside.

Make a white sauce:
2 tablespoons margarine, 1 egg yolk (reserve white)
2 tablespoons flour and 1 cup milk.

Spray a Pyrex/or glass baking dish with cooking spray.
Mix flaked salmon and white sauce in dish.

In separate bowl:
Beat egg white (reserved) until stiff.
Fold carefully into mixture.

Top with crumbled Saltine crackers.
Place 2-3 pats of butter on top of mixture.

Bake @ 350° F. for 30 minutes or until golden brown.
Serve with: Baked potatoes and broccoli

Note - This meal is quick, easy and particularly light.
Be prepared to get rave reviews.

Turkey Paprika over Rice

Arcade Coffee & Sandwich Shoppe
Curt and Terry Koch

2 cups cubed turkey
½ cup (½ stick butter)
1 medium chopped onion
¼ cup Wondra flour
1 teaspoon salt
2 cups milk
3 teaspoons paprika
1 cup sour cream

Cooked Rice

Melt butter in large skillet, over medium heat.
Add onion and cook until tender.
Blend in flour and salt.
Remove from heat and gradually add milk, stirring constantly.
Cook until mixture thickens.
Reduce heat and stir in paprika.
Add turkey and simmer 5 minutes.
Stir in sour cream and heat thoroughly.

Ladle over hot cooked rice.

Serves 6

Note - This is a great use of left-over turkey.

Quick Tuna-Potato Casserole

Arcade Coffee & Sandwich Shoppe
Curt and Terry Koch

2 (4-ounce) packages instant mashed potatoes
1 can cream of mushroom soup
1 (7-ounce) package premium tuna
1 cup shredded cheddar cheese

Pre-heat oven to 350° F.

Prepare mashed potatoes according to package directions.
Set aside.
Spread tuna onto bottom of casserole dish.
Pour undiluted mushroom soup over top of tuna.
Spoon prepared mashed potatoes on top of tuna mixture.
Sprinkle shredded cheese on top.

Cover casserole and Bake @ 350° for 15-20 minutes.

Serves 2-4

Note -There is a diverse selection of seasoned mashed potatoes on the market today. Use your favorite variety.

Terry uses Roasted Garlic for a *Loaded-Baked-Potato* Flavor.

LASAGNA
Beth Rudolph

1 lb Italian sausage (or Jimmy Dean regular sausage)
2 cloves garlic, minced (or the equivalent of minced garlic)
1 tablespoon basil
1½ teaspoons salt

1 One-pound can (2 cups) tomatoes
2 (6-ounce) cans (1½ cups) tomato paste
1 can Tomato sauce

10-ounces lasagna noodles (about 8 noodles)
3 cups fresh Ricotta cheese
½ cup grated Parmesan or Romano cheese
4 tablespoons parsley flakes

5 beaten eggs
1 teaspoon, salt
½ teaspoon pepper
1 lb thinly sliced mozzarella cheese

Brown meat slowly; drain excess fat.
Add next 6 ingredients.
Simmer uncovered 30 minutes or longer, stirring occasionally.

Cook noodles in boiling, salted water, until tender; drain; rinse. Combine remaining ingredients, except Mozzarella cheese. Place half the noodles in a 13x9x2-inch baking dish; spread with half the ricotta cheese filling; add half the Mozzarella cheese and half the meat sauce.

Repeat layers.

Bake @ 375° F. for about 30 minutes.
Let stand 10 minutes before cutting in squares – filling will set slightly. Serves:12.

Note - You may pre-assemble this Lasagna; refrigerate. Be sure to allow an additional 15 minutes or so longer in the oven. Garlic and basil can be adjusted to taste.

Bowties, Sausage & Cream

Elizabeth Ezekiel

2 tablespoons olive oil
1 lb sweet Italian sausages
½ teaspoon dried red pepper flakes
½ cup diced onion
3 cloves garlic, minced
28-ounce can Italian Plum tomatoes, chopped and drained
1½ cup whipping cream
½ teaspoon salt

In skillet, heat oil over medium heat.
Add Italian sausage and red pepper flakes.
Cook until sausage is light brown. (about 7 minutes)
Add drained and chopped tomatoes.
Add whipping cream and salt.
Simmer 4 minutes.

Cook Bowtie pasta until tender, but firm.
Spoon sauce over pasta.
Sprinkle with Parmesan cheese.

Serves: 4-6

Note - Every time Elizabeth serves this wonderful dish to her dinner guests, they always rave... and they ask for the recipe.

Bicycling Bob's Black Bean Soup
Bicycling Bob Dioguardi

1 lb ground beef
1 cup brown rice
2 (19-ounce) black beans
1 can chopped chilies
Olive oil
Salt
Cayenne pepper
Water
½ cup chopped onions

Brown ground beef and onions in olive oil.
Add black beans and chilies.
Salt to taste.
Stir in brown rice.
Add water as needed for desired consistency.
Add cayenne pepper to taste.
Simmer until completely done and rice has plumped to size.

Makes 8 quarts

All ingredients may be increased or decreased according to the number of people you need to serve. Make a little or make a lot... This recipe is a tried and true favorite.

Serve with Hoagie rolls or Italian bread for dunking.

Note - Bicycling Bob Dioguardi writes a weekly column in The Lake Wales News.

Breakfast Lasagna

Jeanine Merritt

6 slices bread
1½ cup milk
1¼ teaspoon dry mustard
1 teaspoon salt
6 eggs
6 oz. medium, shredded cheddar cheese
½ lb breakfast sausage, (cooked/drained)

Pre-heat oven to 350° F.

Line a 9x12-inch baking dish with bread slices.
In bowl, mix eggs, milk and seasonings.
Pour mixture over bread.
Top with crumbled sausage.
Sprinkle cheddar cheese over top.

Bake for 30-40 minutes.

Serves: 6-8

Note - Breakfast Lasagna is a Merritt family tradition.
Jeanine has served this dish on Christmas mornings for many years and she notes that her girls especially look forward to it.

Hahn's Macaroni & Cheese Casserole

Dot Hahn

2 cups elbow macaroni, cooked
2 cups grated Sharp cheddar cheese
(the sharper the cheese, the better the casserole)
3 eggs
1 quart milk
1 teaspoon salt

Boil macaroni for 10 minutes-Drain.
In casserole dish - layer macaroni and cheese.
Macaroni first - end with cheese on top.

Beat eggs well.
Add milk and salt.
Pour mixture over layered macaroni and cheese.
Dot generously with butter or margarine.
(Use a fork to 'prick' the macaroni so milk will penetrate.)

Place casserole in COLD oven.
Bake at 325° F. for 45 minutes.
Then turn up heat to 400° F.
Bake another 5 minutes or until top is brown.

Note - If in a hurry...place under broiler, but watch carefully so as not to burn.

Chicken Tettrazzini

Dot Hahn

1 box spaghetti, cooked
4 cups chicken, diced
½ cup pimentos
½ cup chopped bell pepper
2 cans cream of mushroom soup
1 cup chicken broth
¼ teaspoon salt
½ teaspoon pepper
1 large onion, chopped
¾ lb grated cheese
1 tablespoon Worcestershire sauce
Chopped almonds

Mix together, (reserve a little cheese for topping.)
Place in 9 x12 inch casserole dish.
Sprinkle with remaining cheese.

Bake @ 350° F. for approximately 25 minutes, or until bubbly.

Note - This dish has made an appearance at family dinners and backyard picnics many times...and is always very good.

"Hahn-Made" Taco Pizza

James R. Hahn

1 ready-to-bake Pizza Dough
1 lb lean ground beef
1 package Old El Paso taco seasoning mix
1 can refried beans
1 can tomato sauce

Toppings:
Shredded lettuce
Can of diced tomatoes (with green pepper and onions)
Medium hot salsa
Shredded Mexican cheese
Three Cheese ranch dressing
Salt and pepper

Bake pizza dough in pan according to package directions.
(Usually about 6-7 minutes until pizza dough is done.)
Allow to cool 2 minutes.
In skillet, brown ground beef with Taco seasoning mix, cooking until beef is done. Mix together the refried beans and tomato sauce as needed to make a rich and thick consistency. Spread sauce onto pizza dough.

Add toppings in the following order:
Shredded lettuce / Diced tomatoes / Medium salsa / Shredded Mexican cheese / Three cheese ranch dressing
Salt and pepper to taste / Hot sauce (if needed)
Slice with pizza wheel and serve immediately.

Note - This is my artistic husband's own creative recipe for Taco Pizza. It is our all-time favorite. We both love it.

"The Rembrandt" Wrap

James R. Hahn

6 hard-boiled eggs
Mayo (to taste and consistency)
1 teaspoon dill
1 teaspoon prepared mustard
Salt and pepper to taste
Texas Pete hot sauce

Mash, pre-cooked, hard-boiled eggs.
Blend in mayo, dill, mustard, salt, and pepper.
Spread mixture onto center of wrap.
Sprinkle hot sauce to taste and fold wrap.

This egg salad wrap is now being served at the Arcade Sandwich & Coffee Shoppe where it is presented with an orange slice twist and sliced strawberries on the side.
The *piece de resistance* is a Hershey Kiss.

What's in a name?

My husband ...James R. Hahn, has his art studio in the historic Rhodesbilt Arcade. Across the hall, are our friends Curt and Terry Koch, owners of the Arcade Coffee & Sandwich Shoppe. Curt, who has a nickname for everyone in town, (I am *not* exaggerating) dubbed my artist-husband, *Rembrandt...* and the name stuck. Upon learning that *the artist* was partial to a hot and spicy version of egg salad, Curt added this new wrap to their menu and called it *...The Rembrandt.*

So if you get hungry while visiting downtown Lake Wales, stop in the coffee shop to say hello, and ask for *The Rembrandt.*

International

Tres Jolie éclairs

Jessica K. Bray - Head Pastry Chef

Pate Choux Shells

8½ - ounces water
3½ - ounces unsalted butter
¼ teaspoon salt
¼ teaspoon sugar
1 cup all-purpose flour
4 eggs

In medium saucepan, bring water, butter, salt, and sugar, to a rapid boil.
Remove from heat. Add flour, all at once. Stir until a firm ball forms.
Add eggs, one at a time, stirring briskly until mixture is dry, before adding each additional egg.

Spoon mixture into a decorating bag fitted with a large open star tip, and pipe 12 éclair sized lines. (about 6-inches long)

The dough can also be dropped by spoonfuls and then shaped with a knife on an ungreased cookie sheet.

Bake @ 400° F. for 30-40 minutes, until well browned.

Use a skewer to poke holes into each end and push aside the inside dough, while the shells are still warm.
Fill the cooled shells with your choice of sweetened whipped pastry or Bavarian cream.

Dip tops in warm ganache or sprinkle with powered sugar.

Chocolate Ganache

Jessica K. Bray

4½-ounces Imported Semi-Sweet Chocolate
4½-ounces heavy cream
1-ounce granulated sugar
1-ounce unsalted butter

Add the sugar to the heavy cream, in a medium saucepan. Bring to a slight boil, over low heat.

While the cream is heating, fine chop the chocolate.
Add the chopped chocolate to the hot cream, and swirl in the pan gently, until the chocolate is mostly dissolved.

The mixture will separate.
Use a whisk and stir, in very small circles, in the middle of the pan, until all chocolate is incorporated.

DO NOT WHISK AIR INTO THE MIXTURE.

Cut the butter into 3 chunks and add one piece at a time, incorporating each piece fully with the whisk between each addition.

Cool to room temperature and refrigerate.

Pastry Cream
Jessica K. Bray

4½ cups regular milk
4 egg yolks
8-ounces granulated sugar
2-ounces all-purpose flour
1½-ounce corn starch
1 tablespoon Light Rum or Grand Marnier

Set aside 3-ounces of milk, and pour the rest into a medium saucepan.
Add 2-ounces of sugar and bring the milk to a slight boil over medium heat.
In a large bowl, sift together the remaining sugar, flour and corn starch.
In a small bowl, whisk the set aside milk into the egg yolks.
Add the egg mixture to the dry ingredients and mix well.
Add hot milk, about ¼ cup at a time. Whisk until a medium paste is formed.
Pour the paste slowly into the boiling milk, stirring constantly.
Bring the mixture to a full rolling boil and continue heating for 1 minute.
Remove saucepan from heat and stir until slightly cooled.

Add the rum or liqueur and stir well.

Pour the cream into a bowl and cover the surface with plastic wrap, leaving no air between the surface of the pastry cream.

Refrigerate.

<u>Bavarian Cream</u>
Jessica K. Bray

21-ounces heavy cream
9-ounces pastry cream
Vanilla
Sugar

Whip the heavy cream, on medium speed, until extremely thick.
Whisk the pastry cream until it is very smooth.
Fold pastry cream into the whipped cream.

Add additional vanilla and/or sweetener to taste.

To use the Bavarian cream for éclair filling, allow it to set in the refrigerator for 1 hour before using.

Jessica learned the base recipes for éclairs, from Chef Xavier Cotte of Le Cordon Bleu School, when she studied with him in Paris, France.

While the ingredients are essentially the same, Jessica modified some proportions and techniques to accommodate American taste and the home kitchen.

Note - Serve this recipe to family and friends just once, and you'll understand why it is the most requested pastry at Tres Jolie.

English Cheese, Onion & Bacon Pie

Stuart Avenue Café

Jacqui Johnson

1 lb chopped onions
1 lb grated Cheddar cheese
1 lb bacon, cut up
6 eggs
A little milk (Jacqui's translation)
2 (Pre-baked) pie crusts

Sauté chopped onions and bacon.
In pre-baked pie crust, put a layer of cheese, onion, and bacon.
Repeat layers until all ingredients are used.

Beat the eggs together with a "little milk" and pour mixture over the cheese, onion, and bacon.
Put second pastry crust over top.
Brush top of pastry crust with a "little egg and milk" mixture.

Bake @ 350° F. until pie crust is golden brown.

Note - Jacqui's dad made this quiche-like dish for her, and served it with baked beans and French Fries. Jacqui also likes this pie served cold, with a salad.

For a large party or special gathering, Jacqui bakes this dish in a large pan and cuts the pie into small squares for serving.

English Scones
Stuart Avenue Café
Jacqui Johnson

4 ounces flour
2 ounces currants
2 ounces sugar
2 ounces butter, softened
1 medium egg
Small amount of milk (per Jacqui)

Sift flour 2 times.
Add butter, and knead with your fingers, until mixture is the consistency of bread crumbs.
Place mixture in blender. Pulse for a few seconds.
In mixing bowl, add sugar and currants.
Add egg (and a little milk.)
Form into a ball.

Roll mixture out onto a floured surface.
Using a cookie cutter or glass, cut out 6-8 scones.

Bake @ 350° F. until scones are golden brown.

Serve with: Afternoon Tea.

Note - These are the scones that Jacqui serves at the Stuart Avenue Café, using her basic scone mix. I have had the pleasure of eating these scones on many occasions, and every time, Jacqui does an outstanding job. She gets many calls from her regular customers requesting these authentic English treats.

Jacqui's Pineapple Cake

Stuart Avenue Café
Jacqui Johnson

1 box Yellow Cake mix
½ cup oil
3 eggs
2 cans (20-ounce) crushed pineapple, undrained
¼ cup water
1 (8-ounce) container Cool Whip
2 small packages Vanilla instant pudding

Pre-heat oven to 350° F.

Mix together: yellow cake mix, oil, eggs, water, and 1 can of crushed pineapple. Blend well.

Lightly grease a 9x13-inch baking dish.
Pour cake mixture into prepared baking dish.
Bake for 40 minutes, or until cake is golden brown.

Icing:
Mix together Cool Whip, pudding mix, and the remaining can of crushed pineapple.
Blend for approximately 3 minutes.
Spoon topping onto top of cake.

Refrigerate.

Note - This is a recipe Jacqui acquired from her friend, Janet. It is one of Jacqui's favorites. When Jacqui makes this dessert, she bakes her cake "from scratch." This cake keeps well in the refrigerator.

English Scouse

Stuart Avenue Café
Jacqui Johnson

1 lb mince (ground beef, to us Yanks)
1 lb chopped onion
5 lbs potatoes
1 lb carrots
Beef stock
Water

Sauté mince (beef) and onions.
Add carrots and potatoes, adding enough water to cover all vegetables. Add beef stock.
Boil until vegetables are soft.
Mash vegetables until mixture goes to "mush".

Serve with: Hot French bread... on a cold night.

In England, Scouse was originally made from leftovers from Sunday dinner and was served for Tea on Monday night. Jacqui believes that this recipe originated in Wales.

Scouse is Jacqui's comfort food. She makes it when she is feeling down, or if she is missing her children, who still live in England.

Note - Jacqui, we are so sorry that you miss your kids, but we're thrilled for the scouse. Cheerio!

Boiled Fruit Cake

Stuart Avenue Café
Jacqui Johnson

1 cup water
4 cups mixed fruit
1 cup sugar
¾ cup butter
2 cups all-purpose flour
1 teaspoon baking soda
1 teaspoon All-Spice
2 eggs, beaten

Pre-heat oven to 300° F.

Grease a 9x5-inch loaf pan.
Line with parchment paper or aluminum foil.

In saucepan: combine water, fruit, sugar and butter.
Bring to a a boil, over medium heat, stirring occasionally.
Continue to boil for approximately 10 minutes.
In large bowl, sift together flour, All-Spice and baking soda.
Add fruit mixture. Stir until well blended.
Add eggs and mix thoroughly.

Pour cake mixture into prepared loaf pan.

Bake for 90 minutes.

Let cake cool before removing from pan.

Note - This is Jacqui's original English recipe. All-Spice is known as Mix- spice in England, so its name was changed in this unusual recipe for Boiled Fruit Cake.

Balinese Lamb Chops
Stuart Avenue Café
Jacqui Johnson

Olive oil cooking spray
1 onion, finely chopped
2 tablespoons crunchy peanut butter
1 tablespoon sweet chili sauce
270 ml can coconut milk
8 Lamb Chump Chops*

Pre-heat oven to 350° F.

Heat a non-stick frying pan, over medium heat.
Spray olive oil and cook onions until tender.
Add peanut butter, sweet chili and coconut milk.
Stir until well combined and bring to a boil.

Arrange chops, in a single layer, in oven-proof dish.
Pour sauce over lamb chops. Turn chops to coat both sides.

Bake, uncovered, for 35 minutes, or until chops are cooked through.

Serve with: egg noodles or steamed bok choy.
Serves: 8

*Note - *Chump chops are large chops to us Yanks. Jacqui says you can substitute chicken or use pork chops in this recipe.*

Crab Supper Pie

Shirley Russell Hopp

1 cup shredded, natural Swiss cheese
1 (9-inch) unbaked pie crust
1 (7½-ounce) tin of crabmeat, drained/flaked
2 sliced green onions, with tops
3 beaten eggs
1 cup light cream
½ teaspoon salt
½ teaspoon grated lemon peel
¼ teaspoon dry mustard
Dash of Mace
¼ cup sliced almonds

Sprinkle cheese evenly over bottom of pastry shell.
Top with crabmeat. Sprinkle with green onions.

Combine eggs, cream, salt, lemon peel, dry mustard, and mace.

Pour mixture over crabmeat.

Top with almonds.

Bake @ 325° F. for about 45 minutes, or until set.

Remove from oven. Let stand 10 minutes before serving.

Serves: 6

Note - Crab Pie Supper is of German Ethnicity.
It is wonderful served with a fresh salad for lunch.

Cabo Taco Casserole

Jeff McGee

Taco meat:
1 lb ground beef/chicken
1 package taco seasoning mix

Taco batter:
½ cup cornmeal
¾ cup all-purpose flour
2 envelopes rapid-rise yeast
1 tablespoon sugar
¾ cup milk
3 tablespoons corn oil
1 egg
Salt and pepper to taste

Toppings:
1 cup crushed Corn Chips
1 cup Mexican cheese
1 cup Salsa

Brown meat in skillet-drain. Add taco seasoning, mix well. Set aside. Mix batter ingredients together.

Pour into an 8x8-inch baking dish which has been lightly coated with cooking spray. Top batter with taco meat.
Pour salsa over meat mixture.
Sprinkle with shredded cheese and crushed Corn Chips.

Do not pre-heat oven.
Place baking dish in **cold** oven and set to 350° F.
Bake for approximately 30 minutes, or until done.

Mexican Quiche
Jose J. Ferrar

¼ cup flour
4 eggs
1 can whole-corn
¼ cup Jalapeño pepper
10-ounce package shredded cheese
¾ cup cottage cheese
2 ounces pimentos
½ cup chopped onion
Salt and pepper to taste

Beat eggs for 1 minute.
Combine remaining ingredients into eggs. Mix well.

Bake uncovered @ 350° F. for approximately 30 minutes.

Costa Rican Tres Leches Cake
K Hahn

1 package yellow cake mix
1 package instant vanilla pudding mix
1 cup vegetable oil
4 eggs

Pre-heat oven to 350° F
Coat a 13x9-inch baking dish with cooking spray.
Place dry cake mix and pudding mix in bowl.
Add vegetable oil and 4 eggs. Mix until well blended.
Pour batter into dish and bake for approximately 30-35 minutes
until cake springs back when pressed in center.

Milk Syrup:

1 can sweetened condensed milk
1 can evaporated milk
1 cup heavy whipping cream
1 teaspoon vanilla extract
Option: 1 tablespoon Coffee Liqueur/or Rum

Whisk together condensed milk, evaporated milk, whipping cream, vanilla and coffee liqueur.

Allow cake to cool and pierce with fork tines all over top.
Ladle milk syrup over cake, allowing cake to soak up all the syrup a little at a time.

Use all syrup.
Cover loosely with plastic wrap and refrigerate for 2 hours.

Author's Note- My husband and I lived in Costa Rica for a year. This was our favorite Central American dessert. This one has been simplified using cake mix ala Norte Americano style. It is very rich and sweet. The Spanish name Tres Leches literally means, three milks.

A TRADITIONAL UKRAINIAN CHRISTMAS

In every Ukrainian home, where national customs are practiced, a sheaf of wheat is as much a part of the decorations, as is the Christmas Tree. Farming is the chief livelihood in the Ukraine. A sheaf of wheat is symbolic of the hope that next years' crop will be bountiful. Wisps of hay are spread under the family's dinner table, as well as under their embroidered tablecloths, to represent the manager where Christ was born.

Christmas Eve is an important part of the Christmas season. The Ukrainian home is redecorated and rearranged days ahead of time. With the first evening star, the family members take their places at the dinner table. There is also a place set for any family member who has passed on. Ukrainian women prepare a meatless meal, consisting of 12 different dishes, symbolic of the 12 apostles.
All members of the family partake of at least a portion of each dish served.

Borsch

Irene Nakoneczny j

1 cup grated carrots
1 cup diced celery
2 cups grated beets
1 cup shredded cabbage
½ cup mushrooms
2 medium onions, chopped fine
6½ cups cold water, or stock
2 cups tomato soup
2 tablespoons flour
3 tablespoons butter
Salt & Pepper to taste
1 tablespoon lemon juice (optional)

Mix carrots, celery, beets, and 1 chopped onion with the water. Add salt and pepper and simmer for half an hour.

Sauté chopped onions in butter until transparent.
Add cabbage and mushrooms.

Simmer about 5 minutes. Add to the borsch.

Cook vegetables until tender.
Stir in tomato soup and lemon juice.
Dissolve the flour in ¼ cup of cold water.
Add to borsch.

Note - This recipe for Borsch was passed down to Irene from her mother-in-law. It is served with small, triangular-shaped bits of dough, filled with mushrooms, fish, and Pyrohy, with mushroom gravy.

Miniature dumplings may be added to the borsch.

Sauté 1 small onion in 1 tablespoon butter.
Add ¼ cup finely chopped mushrooms, a pinch of salt and pepper, and 1 tablespoon of cracker crumbs. Stir well.

Using the pyrohy dough, make several miniature pyrohy by placing a small portion of the mushroom filling on each small square of dough. Pinch edges together. Boil in salted water for 5 minutes. Remove from water and pop into the borsch.

PYROHY

3 cups flour
1 cup warm water
2 tablespoons cooking oil
1 egg
1 teaspoon salt

Beat egg, add oil and water. Mix with flour and salt.
Knead well to make soft dough. Let stand, covered, for about 10 minutes.
Roll out dough (thin as for pie crust) on floured board.

Cut into small squares. Place a little of the filling on each square. Fold over into a triangle and pinch the edges together well. Drop into boiling, salted water for 10 minutes.
Drain and rinse with cold water to prevent pyrohy from sticking together. Drain well. Sprinkle melted butter over pyrohy.

Serve with: Onions sautéed in butter, or sour cream with chopped green onions.

Optional Filling for Pyrohy:

- Mashed potatoes, seasoned and mixed with cottage cheese.
- ½ lb Velveeta cheese mixed into about 4 cups of hot mashed potatoes, seasoned to taste.
- Sauerkraut with pieces of chopped bacon.
- Cottage cheese mixed with an egg and pinch of salt.
- Any desired fruit, mixed with a bit of sugar.
- Or, as Irene says..."Whatever strikes your fancy."

Note - Irene hails from the Ukraine. She represents the diversity we have in our Downtown, and exemplifies the universal blending of Main Street Flavors.

The above recipes are dedicated to Irene's mother-in-law, E. Nakonecznyj, who never had the chance to meet her grandchildren.

Slow Cooker

Tips For Slow Cookers

1. Use a non-stick cooking spray to lightly mist the inside of the cooker. Slow cooker bowl liners are now available. Just toss away after each use.

2. To ensure that chicken or beef is completely done, place meat in microwave for a few minutes prior to slow cooking.

3. Skim fat from cooking liquid when done.

4. Resist stirring while cooking. Heat is lost when the lid is removed, and vegetables can break apart and become mushy with repeated stirring.

5. When cooking seafood recipes, it is better to add fish to the slow cooker the last hour or so of cooking.

6. Slow cooking intensifies the flavor of spices such as chili powder and garlic. Use spices sparingly.

7. *Dried herbs* may lessen in intensity. Adjust seasoning at the end of cooking. When using *fresh herbs*, toss them in at the end of cooking for best results.

8. Less tender cuts of meat and poultry are best suited for slow cooking. Use pork or lamb shoulder, beef brisket, chuck roast or chicken/turkey legs and thighs.

9. Sprinkle meat and poultry with flour and brown in skillet before slow cooking, for a richer flavor in soups and stews. Scrape browned bits from skillet and add to cooker to thicken sauce and enhance flavors.

10. For even cooking, always fill slow cooker more than halfway full, but never fill cooker to the brim. Leave about two inches of space between food and lid.

11. You can prep most recipes the night before. Pre-measure ingredients, cut, dice, trim meats, etc. In the A.M. just toss everything in and turn on the slow cooker.

12. Pre-mix and measure recipe ingredients and store in freezer bags to have on hand for an added convenience.

13. If more liquid is produced than desired in your recipe, here is a good tip: Remove solids from cooker with slotted spoon or spatula, turn temperature to High and cook, uncovered, until liquid is reduced to desired consistency.

14. You can buy ready-made slow cooker meals and toss the entire contents into your cooker, flip the switch... and dinner is ready when you are.

Ginger Pork Roll-Ups

Randall Johnson

2½ lbs boneless pork loin roast
3 tablespoons grated ginger
3 tablespoons honey
¼ cup soy sauce
3 cups coleslaw mix
2 tablespoons rice vinegar

12 warmed flour tortillas

Mix ginger and honey in slow cooker.
Add pork and turn to coat with honey mixture.

Cover and cook on Low 6-8 hours or until pork is tender.
Remove pork from slow cooker.
Using 2 forks, shred pork into fine pieces.
Return shredded pork to slow cooker.
Stir in soy sauce.

In separate bowl: Toss coleslaw mix with rice vinegar until well mixed. Set aside.

Spoon meat mixture down center of each warm tortilla.
Top with coleslaw and roll up.

Makes 12 wraps

Note - For a different flavor, use regular coleslaw dressing instead of the rice vinegar.

Spicy Chili-Pork Tacos

Randall Johnson

2 lbs boneless pork center loin roast
(cut pork into small strips)
1 can diced tomatoes
1 can chopped green chilies
½ teaspoon hot sauce
2 teaspoons ground red chilies
Seasoning to taste

12 taco shells
¾ cup shredded cheese
1½ cups shredded lettuce

Combine pork strips, red and green chilies, tomatoes, hot sauce and seasonings.
Pour mixture into slow cooker.
Cover and cook on Low for 8-9 hours or until pork is tender.

Spoon pork mixture into warmed taco shells.
Top with cheese and lettuce.

Note - Give your taco an ethnic flavor by serving with a green salad with avocado slices. Top with sour cream, guacamole and your favorite salsa.

New Orleans Bayou Gumbo
Sam Hicks

½ lb hot smoked pork sausage, diced into chunks
3 tablespoons vegetable oil
2 cups frozen cut okra
1 large chopped onion
1 large chopped bell pepper
2 cloves garlic, finely chopped
3 tablespoons all-purpose flour
¼ teaspoon cayenne pepper
¼ teaspoon black pepper
1 can diced tomatoes, undrained
1½ cup regular long-grained rice
3 cups water
1 package (12-ounce) frozen, cooked shrimp
(peeled, de-veined, rinsed and drained)

Heat oil on medium heat and stir in flour.
Cook for several minutes, stirring constantly, until mixture turns reddish brown. Pour flour/oil mix into cooker.
Stir in remaining ingredients (except rice, water and shrimp.)
Cover and cook on Low for 7-8 hours.
In separate pot, cook rice in water until rice is tender.
While rice is cooking, stir shrimp into gumbo mixture.
Cover and cook on Low for approximately 20 minutes.

Serve Gumbo over a platter of rice. Serves 6

Note - There are as many gumbo recipes as there are cooks, but authentic, Creole style gumbo starts with a rich roux (oil and flour base) and uses okra as a thickener.
This shrimp gumbo is standard fare in New Orleans.

Mediterranean-Style Pot Roast
Ruth Benson

3 lbs boneless beef chuck roast
1 tablespoon Italian seasoning
1 clove garlic, minced
½ cup sun dried tomatoes, chopped and drained
½ cup beef broth
½ cup pitted black olives
½ cup frozen pearl onions
Salt and pepper to taste

In skillet, cook beef until brown.
Sprinkle with Italian seasoning, garlic, salt and pepper.
Place beef in bottom of cooker, seasoned side up.
Arrange tomatoes and black olives on top of beef.
Top with onions and beef broth.

Cover and cook on Low for 6 hours, or until beef is tender.
Remove beef from cooker and allow to cool 10 minutes.
Slice beef and ladle onions and broth over meat.

Serves 8-10

Note - Try Pizza seasoning instead of Italian.
In addition to the usual spices in Italian cuisine, such as basil garlic and oregano, pizza seasoning has a nice blend of bell peppers as well.

Serve With: Garlic mashed potatoes or potato skins and a garden salad.

<u>Honey-Glazed Barbeque Pork Roast</u>

Gabe Phillip

3 lbs boneless pork shoulder roast
1 cup Barbeque sauce, divided
¼ cup honey
1 bag baby carrots, cut up
3 tablespoons balsamic vinegar
1 cup frozen whole-kernel corn
¼ cup all-purpose flour
1 teaspoon seasoned salt
Pepper to taste

Place pork roast in bottom of slow cooker.
Arrange carrots around and on top of pork.
Mix ½ of the barbeque sauce, honey, vinegar and seasoned salt in a small bowl. Pour sauce over pork and carrots.
Cover and cook on Low for 8-10 hours or until pork is done.
Remove pork and vegetables from slow cooker, placing on platter and cover to keep warm.

Mix the rest of the barbeque sauce with the flour.
Gradually pour into the juices in the slow cooker.
Cover and cook on High for 15 minutes, stirring frequently, allowing sauce to thicken.
Stir corn into mixture. Cover and cook 5 minutes longer.
Ladle sauce over pork and vegetables. Serves 6.

Note - The flavor is greatly influenced by the type BBQ sauce used for this glaze. Experiment to find your favorite.

Though dark and rich, balsamic vinegar is aged from the juice of white grapes. A splash of this delightful Italian vinegar adds depth to sauces, soup and stews.

Turkey and Wild-Rice Casserole
Gabe Phillip

1 lb turkey breast tenderloins, cut up
4 slices bacon, cut into small pieces
1 medium chopped onion
2 medium carrots, chopped
1 medium celery stalk, chopped
1 can condensed cream of chicken soup
2½ cups water
2 tablespoons soy sauce
1 cup uncooked wild rice
Salt and pepper to taste

In skillet, cook bacon until crisp.
Stir in turkey, onions, carrots and celery.
Cook until turkey is done and browned.
Arrange turkey mixture in bottom of slow cooker.
Stir in all remaining ingredients.
Cover and cook on Low for 5-6 hours or until wild-rice is tender and liquid is absorbed.

Serves 5

Substitute: Chicken breasts may be used instead of turkey for this recipe.

Note - Wild rice is not actually a rice at all.
It is a long-grain marsh grass that has a chewy texture and a rich, nutty flavor that enhances soups and casseroles.

Chris' Chicken-Mushroom Stroganoff

Chris Golden

1 lb boneless, skinless chicken breasts halves, cut up
1 can condensed cream of chicken soup
1 envelope chicken gravy mix
1 small jar sliced mushrooms, drained
1 bag frozen stew vegetables, thawed and drained
½ cup sour cream
1½ cups Bisquick (original or reduced fat)
¼ cup green onions
½ cup milk

Mix together until smooth, the gravy mix and chicken soup, and pour into slow cooker.
Stir in the chicken, stew vegetables and mushrooms.
Cover and cook on Low for 4 hours or until chicken is done.
Mix together peas and sour cream.
Stir into chicken mixture.
Cover and cook on High for 20 minutes.

Combine Bisquick and green onions and stir in milk until just moistened. Drop dough by tablespoons onto chicken mixture.

Cover and cook on High for 45-50 minutes or until toothpick inserted into center of dumplings comes out clean.

Serves 4

Note - This Stroganoff is an exceptionally rich and creamy dish that features dumplings instead of the traditional noodles.

Vegetable Beef Soup for Slow Cooker

Brittany Ryan

1½ lbs beef stew meat
1 chopped onion
1 chopped bell pepper
2 thinly sliced carrots
1 can whole-kernel corn
2 medium diced potatoes
Salt and pepper to taste
1½ cups water
½ teaspoon dried thyme leaves
2 cans beef broth
2 cans diced tomatoes, undrained
1 can tomato sauce

Mix all ingredients together until thoroughly blended.
Pour into a 3½-to 6-quart slow cooker.
Cover and cook on Low for 8-9 hours.
High heat setting for 4-5 hours, or until vegetables are tender.

Serves 10

Note - Substitute 2 cans of tomatoes with garlic for a different flavor, or use regular tomatoes and add ½ teaspoon of garlic powder.

Old World Chicken Stew

Dan Simmons

1 lb boneless chicken thighs, cut up
2 cups chopped cabbage
½ lb Polish sausage
1 cup chopped carrots
1 medium onion, chopped
2 cloves minced garlic
2 cans chicken broth
1 can condensed cream of mushroom soup
1 cup uncooked wild rice, rinsed and drained

Combine all ingredients (except soup and broth) and pour into bottom of a 3½-to 4-quart slow cooker.
Mix cream of mushroom soup and broth together in a medium size bowl.
Pour soup mixture over meat and vegetables.
Stir gently until blended.
Cover and cook on Low for 7-8 hours, or until chicken is done in center.

Serves 8

Note - Fresh mushrooms can be added to this stew to enhance its rich and hearty flavor.

Slow Cooker Chicken Noodle Soup
Valerie Reynolds

1 lb boneless chicken thighs, cut up
2 medium carrots, chopped
2 medium stalks celery, diced
1 medium chopped onion
1 can chicken broth
1 can diced tomatoes, undrained
1 package frozen peas
Salt and pepper to taste
1 cup frozen egg noodles (from 12-ounce bag)

Spray skillet with cooking spray.
Cook chicken in skillet until golden brown.
Mix chicken with carrots, celery, onion, chicken broth, and tomatoes.
Pour into slow cooker.
Cover and cook on Low for 7 hours, or until chicken is done and no longer pink in center.
Stir in egg noodles and peas.
Cover and cook 15 minutes until noodles are done.

Note - This Chicken Noodle Soup is a real comfort food, served hot and steamy with assorted cheese and crackers.

O'Malley's Mulligan Stew

Brian O'Malley

3 lbs chicken, cup up
(or use legs or thighs)
4 cups tomatoes
2 cups frozen corn
10-ounce package frozen lima beans
½ cup chopped onion
Dash of cayenne pepper
1½ teaspoon salt
Pepper to taste

Place chicken in large cooker. Add water to cover.
Add salt. (hold out other ingredients for now.)
Cover and cook on Low for 2 hours
Add more water if needed at this point.
Add all remaining ingredients.
Simmer 5 hours.

Note - This Mulligan Stew recipe has been in Brian's family for several years and was originally made in a large stock-pot on top of the stove. Brian converted the recipe to slow-cooking which allows him freedom during the day for his other projects. Brian loves how the flavors blend together during the cooking process.

Vinnie's Chicken a la King

Vinnie Prada

1½ lbs boneless, skinless chicken breasts
1 can cream of chicken soup
3 tablespoons flour
9-ounce package frozen soup vegetables (peas, onions, carrots)
½ teaspoon paprika
Salt and pepper to taste

Cut chicken into bite size pieces and place in bottom of slow cooker.

Combine soup, flour, salt and pepper.
Dump over chicken, do not stir.

Cover and cook on High for 2½ hours
or on low for 5½ hours.

Stir in vegetables and paprika.

Cover and cook on High for additional 30 minutes.

Slow Cooker Chicken Pizza Parmesan

Vinnie Prada

6 boneless chicken breast halves
1 cup Italian bread crumbs
1 egg
3-4 tablespoons butter
14-ounce jar of pizza sauce
6 slices Mozzarella cheese
Salt and pepper to taste
Grated Parmesan cheese

Beat egg, salt and pepper.
Dip chicken in egg and coat with bread crumbs.
Sauté chicken in butter and arrange in bottom of cooker.
Pour pizza sauce over chicken.
Cover and cook on low 6-8 hours.
Layer Mozzarella over top and sprinkle with Parmesan.
Cook additional 15 minutes.

Serve with: Green Salad or Caesar Salad

Pork Chops in Barbeque Bean Sauce

Tina Stevens

6 pork chops
1 Large can barbeque baked beans
Large can crushed pineapple, undrained
½ teaspoon garlic salt
½ cup chopped onions
¼ cup hot sauce
Salt and pepper to taste

Brown pork chops and onions in skillet.
Arrange chops and onions in bottom of slow cooker.
Mix together garlic salt, hot sauce, salt and pepper, and baked beans.
Pour over chops.
Sprinkle pineapple chucks over beans.

Cover and cook on Low for 7-8 hours.

Note - This is a great choice for an outdoor barbeque or a Fourth of July party. This recipe feels like summer.

Serve with: Coleslaw and some brown-n-serve rolls.

Slow Simmered Kidney Beans

6 slices bacon, diced
½ lb fully-cooked Kielbasa, cut up
4 cans kidney beans, drained
1 28-ounce can diced tomatoes, drained
2 medium sweet red peppers, chopped
1 large chopped onion
1 cup ketchup
½ cup brown sugar
¼ cup maple syrup/molasses
¼ cup honey
1 tablespoon Worcestershire sauce
2 medium red apples, cored and diced
Salt and pepper to taste

In skillet, cook bacon, remove and drain on paper towels.
Add Kielbasa to bacon drippings, cook 5 minutes, set aside.
In slow cooker, combine beans, tomatoes, peppers, onions, ketchup, brown sugar, honey, maple syrup, Worcestershire sauce, salt and pepper.
Stir in bacon and Kielbasa.
Cover and cook on Low for 4-6 hours.
Stir in apples and cook for additional 2 hours, until bubbly.

Makes 16 servings.

Note - The apples, honey, brown sugar, and maple syrup blend together to give these beans a rich, sweet flavor.

Chunky Chili
Mark Hammock

1 lb ground beef
1 lb pork sausage
2 cans diced tomatoes, undrained
2 cans diced tomatoes with chilies, undrained
1 large chopped onion
1 large chopped green pepper
1 envelope taco seasoning
Hot sauce (optional)
Salt and pepper to taste

Cook beef, sausage, onions and peppers in skillet.

Stir in all remaining ingredients.

Transfer to slow cooker.

Cover and cook on High for 4-5 hours.

Country Corn Chowder
Pam B.

2 (10-ounce) packages frozen corn
16-ounce can cream-style corn
½ cup chopped onion
2 cups diced potatoes
1 teaspoon sugar
1 teaspoon Worcestershire sauce
1 cup water
Salt and pepper to taste

Sauté onions and potatoes in skillet.

Combine all remaining ingredients, mix well.
Cook on Low for 6-7 hours. (In slow cooker)

On stovetop, cook until vegetables are tender.

Note - Pam got this recipe from her Aunt Ruth, who lives in Charleston, South Carolina. Pam visited her aunt during summer vacation and remembers having this delectable corn chowder at dinner time. It was accompanied by fresh-baked bread, straight from the oven, and a big serving of green beans from the backyard garden.

Aunt Ruth's Chicken Stew

Pam B.

6 boneless, skinless chicken breasts
3 cups diced zucchini
1 medium chopped onion
1 cup chopped green pepper
2 cloves garlic
3 medium tomatoes, diced
1 can tomato paste
¾ cup water
Salt and pepper to taste
(Optional spices include basil, thyme, oregano, tarragon, etc.)

Cut chicken into cubes and brown in skillet.
Transfer to cooker.
In same skillet, sauté onions, peppers, and zucchini.
Place in cooker on top of chicken pieces.
Add tomatoes, tomato paste, water and spices.

In Slow Cooker-Cook on Low for 4 hours or until vegetables are tender.
On Stovetop, cook until chicken is done and vegetables are tender.

Note - Pam remembers gathering herbs from her aunt's garden. She suggests trying different spices each time you make this stew, that way you will find your own perfect blend of flavors.

Miscellaneous

Caramel Apple Dip
Ralph Morrow

1 package cream cheese, softened
1 cup brown sugar
1 teaspoon vanilla
½ cup chopped pecans or peanuts

In bowl, combine cream cheese, brown sugar and vanilla.
Beat until a creamy consistency is reached.
Stir in pecans or peanuts.

Refrigerate to chill.
Serve with: Sliced apples.
Substitute walnuts for pecans or peanuts.

Chocolate Fruit Dip
Ralph Morrow

1 package cream cheese, softened
¼ cup chocolate syrup
1 (7-ounce) jar Marshmallow Cream

Assorted fruit such as:
Strawberries, banana slices or pineapple chunks

Blend together cream cheese and chocolate syrup until smooth and creamy.
Fold in Marshmallow Cream.

Cover and refrigerate until ready to serve.
Serve with: Assorted fresh fruit or marshmallows.

Nell G's Homemade Barbeque Sauce

Nell Gheesling

Large 32-oz bottle Catsup
2 cups red vinegar
4 tablespoons seasoned salt
3 tablespoons black pepper
8 tablespoons Worcestershire sauce
8 tablespoons sugar
8 tablespoons prepared mustard
4 tablespoons lemon juice

Mix all ingredients and heat.
Simmer for 30 minutes, stirring occasionally.

Cool and then pour into bottles.
Will keep without refrigeration.

Makes 3½ pints.

For onion flavored barbeque sauce:
Sauté 1 large onion in butter and add to recipe.

Note - This is the best tasting BBQ sauce. The flavor enhances the taste of any meat. My dad used this sauce when he cooked on the grill. We loved it on chicken and pulled pork for BBQ sandwiches.

Nell's Banana Jam
Nell Gheesling

12 large bananas, medium ripe
5 cups sugar
1½ cups orange juice
¾ cup lemon juice
1 teaspoon vanilla

In a large, heavy pot, combine all ingredients.
Stir over moderate heat until sugar dissolves.
Boil rapidly for 10 minutes.
Reduce heat and simmer.

Stir frequently for 15 minutes, until thickened.
Remove from heat and ladle into canning jars.

Makes 5 pints

This is a recipe my Mom made almost every year. Family and friends looked forward to this unique taste sensation. There is nothing quite like this in the jam and jelly section of your local grocery store.

Note - This topping is good on toast and waffles. You can mix some in with your regular pancake batter for some melt-in-your-mouth banana pancakes!

<u>Nell's Fail-Proof Rice</u>
Nell Gheesling

To make 3 cups of rice:

1 cup uncooked rice
2 cups water
1 teaspoon salt (or to taste)

Bring water to full boil.
Turn temperature to low and cover with lid.
Simmer 14 minutes or until all water is absorbed.

For extra tender rice:
Set aside, covered, for additional 10 minutes.

Note - I remember making rice before I got this recipe from my mom. You know the drill...bring water to boil, add rice, stir, boil, keep stirring, hope and pray to rice god that it wouldn't stick...it always did.

My mom liked using short cuts in the kitchen and she taught me well. You can do something fabulous with the time you save. For me...I'd rather be writing.

Pasta Re-Heat
C. Moon

Basic pasta

1 package angel hair pasta
¼ cup butter
½ cup sour cream
½ cup Ranch Dressing
½ cup grated Parmesan cheese

Cook angel hair pasta according to directions.
Drain and return to pot.
Stir in butter and remaining ingredients.

Re-Heat Ingredients
Ham and broccoli
Chicken, peas, and carrots
Any leftover meats and vegetables

Using any number of leftover ingredients you can turn this pasta recipe into a fast and flavorful main dish.

Just stir in your choice of leftovers and heat through.
Or just open a can of chicken or tuna, add a can of mixed vegetables, and have yourself a quick and easy meal.

Option - Substitute spaghetti or egg noodles.
Also Cheddar/or Swiss is another alternative to Parmesan.
Pop the top on a jar of Alfredo sauce and go to town.

Barry's Barbeque Grilling Sauce

Barry Sykes

1 finely chopped onion
2 tablespoons olive oil
2 cloves garlic
1½ cups apple juice
1 (16-oz) can tomato paste
½ cup vinegar
4 tablespoons brown sugar
¼ cup molasses
2 teaspoons paprika
2 tablespoons Worcestershire sauce
Salt and pepper to taste

In olive oil, sauté onion and garlic until tender.
Stir in apple juice, tomato paste, brown sugar,
molasses, vinegar, paprika, Worcestershire sauce.
Salt and pepper according to taste.
Bring to boiling and reduce heat.

Simmer, uncovered for 30 minutes, until desired
consistency is reached... stirring occasionally.

Brush grilling sauce onto chicken, beef, or pork during the last 10
minutes of grilling for a robust barbeque flavor.

Note - This recipe is easily doubled to make a larger batch/or to bottle and refrigerate for later use.

Desserts

Chalet Suzanne®
Restaurant and Inn

Chalet Suzanne's Orange Aspic Pound Cake

1 package Yellow Cake Mix
1 cup **Chalet Suzanne Orange Aspic** (from13-oz can)
1 package (3¾ oz) Vanilla Instant Pudding (use dry)
4 Eggs
2/3 cup Water
¼ cup Cooking Oil

Heat oven to 325° F. Grease and flour 9-inch Bundt pan.
Beat eggs slightly.

Combine all ingredients in a large mixing bowl. Beat 2 minutes, at medium speed.

Pour into prepared pan.

Bake approximately 45 min. or until wooden pick inserted in center of cake comes out clean.

Cool 10-15 min. before turning cake out onto cake plate.
Cool and glaze.

Glaze

½ cup Orange Aspic (remainder of 13-oz. can)
1 Tbsp. Butter or Margarine
2 cups powered sugar (sifted)
Warm aspic on low heat until thinned.
Drop in butter and stir until melted.
Blend in powered sugar.
Drizzle over cake.

Since the 1950's Chalet Suzanne has produced a line of gourmet soups and sauces. This recipe, using Orange Aspic, is one of the most requested.

Chalet Suzanne's Gateau Cristina

Meringue:
4 egg whites
1½ cups sugar
1/3 cup blanched ground almonds

Pre-heat oven to 250° F. Cut aluminum foil into 4, 8-inch circles and grease each lightly.

Whip egg whites until stiff. Gradually adding sugar and almonds as eggs begin to stiffen.

Place foil rounds on a large baking sheet and spread each evenly with meringue.

Bake for 15 min. or until meringue is dry.

Carefully turn meringues over and bake 5 min. longer.

Chocolate filling:

2 egg whites
½ cup sugar
2 Tablespoons unsweetened cocoa
2 sticks butter, softened
4 ounces semi-sweet chocolate, melted

In the top of a double boiler, over hot (not boiling) water, beat egg whites until foamy.

Gradually add sugar, cocoa, butter, and chocolate, beating until thick and creamy.

Remove from heat and cool.

To assemble gateau:

Place the best meringue layer on the bottom and spread with chocolate.
Top with another meringue, pressing down lightly to make layers fit together.
Spread with chocolate.
Repeat until all meringues are used and the top is liberally coated with chocolate.

Cover and refrigerate for at least 24 hours.

Yields: One 4-layered gateau.

Note - Use decorative tin boxes to store these delectable treats. This creates a special gift... for any occasion.

Calamondin Pie
Shirley Russell Hopp

1 (9-inch) pre-baked pie crust
1 (14-ounce) can condensed milk
3 egg yolks
½ to ¾ cup minced calamondin

Quarter calamondin and remove seeds.
(Using a food processor, mince or finely chop)

Combine all ingredients until smooth.
Pour into pre-baked pie crust.

Bake @ 350° F. for 10 minutes.

Remove from oven. Allow to cool.

Refrigerate until ready to serve. Top with whipped cream.

Serves: 8

Note - Calamondin Pie is a Florida dessert, similar to key-lime pie. This dessert tends to be slightly yellow or orange in color.

<u>Apricot Fold-Overs</u>
Mary Lee Harrell

½ cup butter
4-oz. sharp American cheese, grated (1 cup)
1-1/3 cup sifted all-purpose flour
2 tablespoons water
1 cup dried apricots, chopped
1 cup sugar

Cream butter and cheese until light.
Blend sifted flour into creamed mixture.
Add water and mix well.
Chill 4-5 hours.

Meanwhile, cook apricots according to package directions.
Drain well. Stir sugar into hot fruit.
Cook and stir until mixture boils and becomes smooth.
Cool. Divide chilled dough in half.
Roll each half into a 10-inch square.
Cut dough into 2½- inch squares.
Place 1 teaspoon apricot filling in each square.
Bring up diagonal corners and seal.

Bake @ 375° F. on ungreased cookie sheet for 8-10 minutes.

Servings: 2½ Dozen
Great served with: Coffee...for Brunches and Teas.
<u>These Apricot Fold-Overs are Scrumptious!</u>

Note - Apricot Fold-Overs are a family favorite at Christmas time. The children and grand-children request them each year.
Mary Lee's husband says it's the "only gift he wants."

Fluffy Gloss Icing
Elizabeth Ezekiel

2 egg whites, beaten very stiff
¼ cup sugar
¾ cup Karo syrup
½ teaspoon vanilla [optional]

Beat 2 egg whites until very stiff.
Add sugar and beat again.

Continue beating while slowly pouring in Karo syrup.
Watch for soft peaks to form when beaters are lifted.

Stir in vanilla. (or optional flavoring)

This recipe makes a lot. You never have to worry about
having enough icing to cover the whole cake.

Note - This Fluffy Gloss Icing is quick and easy to prepare, and always comes out great.

Pumpkin Pie Cake
Erica Falchetti

Bottom layer:
1 box yellow cake mix (remove 1 cup and save)
To the remainder add:
1 stick margarine (melted)
1 egg (beaten)

Using a fork, stir until all cake is absorbed. Press this mixture into the bottom of a greased and floured 9x13-inch pan.

Filling:
1 large can of pumpkin
3 eggs
½ cup brown sugar
¼ cup sugar
2/3 cup milk
1 teaspoon cinnamon.
Mix all ingredients together.
Beat well and spread over cake mixture.

Topping:

To the 1 cup of reserved cake mix, add ½ cup sugar.
Mix well, then crumble with a ½ stick of cold butter.
Sprinkle topping over pumpkin mixture.

Bake @ 350° F. for 50-55 minutes. Cool in pan. Serve cold.

Note- -Erica works in the law firm of Weaver & McClendon, and was instrumental in gathering the recipes and feature information about the firm. Thanks, Erica.

Cajun Sheet Cake

Arcade Coffee & Sandwich Shoppe
Curt and Terry Koch

2 cups flour
2 cups sugar
3 sticks butter
10 tablespoons Hershey's Cocoa
2 eggs, slightly beaten
½ cup milk plus 5 tablespoons milk
2 teaspoons vanilla
1 cup water
2 teaspoons cinnamon
1 teaspoon baking soda
Box plus 1 cup powdered sugar

Sift together 2 cups flour and 2 cups sugar into mixing bowl and set aside.
In saucepan, bring to a boil 2 sticks butter, 1 cup water and 6 tablespoons Hershey's cocoa.
Pour boiling mixture over flour and sugar. Mix well.
Add 2 eggs, ½ cup of milk, 1 teaspoon baking soda, cinnamon and vanilla. Mix well.
Pour into a greased 9x13x2-inch cake pan.

Bake @ 400° F for 25 minutes or until done.

While cake is cooling: In saucepan, put 1 stick butter, 5 tablespoons milk, 4 tablespoons cocoa. Heat until just bubbly around edges. Add 1 box and 1 cup powered sugar, and 1 teaspoon vanilla. Mix well and spread icing over warm cake.

Note - Terry made this cake for us to try. The cinnamon gives this cake a very distinctive flavor.

ALMOND JOY CAKE
Ashley Bullard

1 chocolate cake mix (bake by directions on box)

1 cup evaporated milk
1 cup sugar
24 large marshmallows
14-oz coconut
1 to 1½ cups chopped pecans
½ cup evaporated milk
1½ cups milk-chocolate chips
1½ cups sugar
1 stick butter

In saucepan: combine evaporated milk and sugar;
Bring to a boil.
Remove from heat and add 24 large marshmallows.
Stir until completely melted.
Add 14-oz. coconut. Pour over hot cake. Cover completely.

In saucepan: mix sugar, milk and pecans.
Bring to full boil, remove from heat.
Add 1 stick butter and chocolate chips.
Stir until chocolate chips are completely melted.
Pour over cake.

Note - Ashley works in the law firm of Weaver & McClendon, PA. on Park Avenue, in downtown Lake Wales.

Coconut Ice Cream

Jim Weaver
Weaver & McClendon, PA

6 eggs
2 (14-oz) cans of sweetened condensed milk
2 (3.4-oz) pkgs. of Instant vanilla pudding
3½-oz. (half of 7-oz bag) of sweetened coconut flakes
1 (15-oz) can of Cream of Coconut
½ teaspoon of Vanilla extract
½ teaspoon of Coconut extract
1 quart of whole milk

Whip eggs on high for 1 minute.
Add sweetened condensed milk. Whip 1 minute.

Add instant vanilla pudding. Whip 1 minute.

Stir in coconut flakes, cream of coconut, vanilla extract, and coconut extract.

Whip all ingredients for 1 minute.

Pour mixture into an ice cream mixer canister.
Add whole milk (less than a quart) to fill line.

Layer crushed ice and rock salt at 4-inch intervals.

Allow ingredients to churn in ice cream maker.

Yield: 2+ Quarts

Rocky Road S'mores Bars

Robin Baker
Lake Region High School

1 cup margarine, softened
1 cup graham cracker crumbs
1 cup brown sugar
2 cups flour
3 cups mini-marshmallows
1½ cups chocolate chips

Combine the margarine, graham cracker crumbs, brown sugar and flour.
The mixture will be crumbly.
Spray a 9x13-inch pan with non-stick cooking spray.
Pat the graham cracker mixture into the bottom and slightly up the sides of pan.

Sprinkle marshmallows and chocolate chips over the graham cracker mixture.

Bake @ 375° F. for 20 minutes.

Gheesling Family Birthday Cake

Jean Ufret

Cake:

2 cups flour
2/3 cup butter
1½ cups sugar
1 teaspoon vanilla
2 teaspoons baking powder
3 eggs
2/3 cup of milk

Cream butter and sugar.
Add eggs, one at a time.
Add milk and flour, alternately.
Add vanilla.
Beat until smooth.
Bake @ 350° F. for 25 minutes.
Makes 2 layers

Icing:

1 box 10x powered sugar Melt a little butter. Add to small can of evaporated milk. Add a little and stir.
Add milk, as needed, stir until smooth.

Note - Add food coloring to make colored cake, or cocoa for chocolate cake. Every year, for our birthday, this was our special cake. We each had our own traditional color. It never varied ... we never wanted it to.

Family Cake Colors:

Kay- Pink
Wayne-Chocolate
Jean-Light Green

Nell's Homemade Fudge
Jean Ufret

4 cups sugar
10 teaspoons cocoa
2 small cans evaporated milk
12 large marshmallows
2 cups nuts
2 teaspoons vanilla
1 tablespoon butter (after removal from heat)

Boil sugar, cocoa, and milk for 12 minutes, or until temperature reaches the softball stage, using candy thermometer.

Remove from heat.

Add butter, nuts, vanilla, and marshmallows.

Beat quickly, until thick.

Pour mixture into buttered sheet pan, with sides.

Authors note - My sister, Jean, sent me this recipe from her own, personal collection. Mom used this recipe to make her delicious, home-made fudge. This was another one of Nell's "lost recipes"

Christmas Eve Crumb Cake

Mama Lillie

Cake:

1 package Graham cracker crumbs
5 cups sugar
5 eggs
2 sticks margarine
2/3 cup buttermilk
1 cup shredded coconut
2 teaspoons baking powder
1 teaspoon vanilla

Cream together, margarine, sugar and eggs.
Mix graham cracker crumbs and coconut together.
Add baking powder, then add buttermilk and vanilla.
Mix well.
Bake @ 350° F. for 30 minutes. Makes 3 layers

Icing:

1 box 10x powered sugar
1 stick margarine
4 teaspoons canned milk
1 small can crushed pineapple, drained well (reserve juice)

Mix together sugar and softened butter.
Blend in all other ingredients.
If icing is too thick, add some of the reserved pineapple juice.

Author's note - My sister, Jean, made this cake for us every Christmas eve. She got the recipe from our Grandfather's second wife, known to us as "Mama Lillie". This cake is unique because it forms its own outer crust. This was a Yuletide tradition in our home.

Jason's Favorite: Nana's Reese's Candy
Jason Lanford

Bottom layer:
2 sticks margarine, melted
1 box powdered sugar
1 1/3 cup graham cracker crumbs
½ cup peanut butter

Mix together well.
Pat onto cookie sheet.
Chill thoroughly.

Top layer:
1 package (12-oz) chocolate chips
½ cup peanut butter

In sauce pan, stir "top layer" ingredients over medium heat. Mix thoroughly until melted & blended. Let cool, slightly.
Spread on top of peanut butter mixture.
Cut into squares for a mouth-watering treat.

Serves: Jason
Great served with: MORE
Also try: A glass of ice-cold milk

Author's Note - Jason is my brilliant, talented and gifted son. Did I mention how smart he is? This is a truth, not a redundancy. My mother made this addictive candy, especially for Jason, every Christmas Eve. Other, less fortunate families, had to rely on marking the calendar to know when Christmas arrived, but in the Gheesling home, we just waited until the candy was brought out, and it was Holiday High Fives all the way around.

Blue Ribbon Banana Pudding
K Hahn

1 large package vanilla instant pudding
Mix by package directions

Add:
1 can sweetened condensed milk
1 large carton Cool Whip

Vanilla wafers
Bananas

Mix pudding ingredients with condensed milk
Add Cool Whip

Line vanilla wafers around bottom and sides of bowl.
Add sliced bananas.
Top with pudding mixture.

Repeat layers of wafers, bananas and pudding mixture.

Top with additional wafers and refrigerate.

Note - This is the best recipe I have ever tried for Banana Pudding. It is extremely rich and delicious.

Enjoy this scrumptious dessert, guilt free ... Bananas are good for you!

Florence's French Raisin Pie
Florence LaGrone

3 eggs
½ cup melted butter
1½ cups sugar
½ teaspoon allspice
½ teaspoon cinnamon
1 tablespoon vinegar
1 teaspoon vanilla
½ cup rasins
½ cup pecans
¼ teaspoon salt

Mix together all ingredients. Pour into unbaked pie shell.
Bake @ 350 F. for 50 minutes to 1 hour.

Note - This was my grandmother's recipe. This pie always impresses. It looks and tastes decadent.

Griswood Drive Fruit Pizza
Kim on Griswood

1 package refrigerated cookie dough
1 8-ounce package cream cheese
1½ cup of sugar, divided
½ teaspoon vanilla
1 large can chunk pineapple, undrained
4 tablespoons cornstarch

Your choice of fresh fruit:
Sliced strawberries, bananas, kiwis, etc

Soften cookie dough and cream cheese to room temperature.
Spray pizza pan with cooking spray.

Press cookie dough to cover pan.

Bake @ 350° F. for 10-12 minutes.
Allow to cool.

Mix cream cheese with ½ cup of sugar and vanilla until smooth.
Spread over cooled crust. Set aside.

Arrange pineapple chunks and other assorted fruit in a colorful and attractive pattern on top of cream cheese layer.
A circular pattern works well with alternating rows of bananas, kiwis, etc.

Glaze:
Mix pineapple and juice in a 2-cup microwave bowl.
Add 1 cup sugar and 4 tablespoons cornstarch.
Stir with wire whisk to remove lumps.
Microwave high 2-3 minutes until thick and transparent.
Allow to cool.

When pizza is covered with fruit, pour the cooled glaze over the entire surface.
Make sure glaze is spread to cover all fruit, as this will keep fruit fresh and bananas from turning brown.

Cover with plastic wrap and refrigerate.
Cut with pizza wheel when ready to serve.

Note - Kim is a friend and was a neighbor of my sister, Jean. Kim brought this pizza for a summer birthday party and it was descended on... and gone... in a manner of just a few minutes. You should really try this one. It is extremely good.

<u>New York Deli-Style Cheesecake</u>
Kevin and Kelly Haney

4 (8-oz) packages cream cheese, room temperature
1½ cups granulated sugar
½ cup (1 stick) butter, room temperature
3 tablespoons all-purpose flour
3 tablespoons cornstarch
4 eggs, room temperature
1 pint dairy sour cream, room temperature
2 teaspoons vanilla

In a large bowl, with an electric mixer, beat cream cheese and sugar until smooth.
Beat in butter, flour and cornstarch.
Add eggs, one at a time, beating well after each addition.
Blend in sour cream and vanilla.
Pour into a 10-inch spring-form pan.

Bake in pre-heated oven @ 325° F. for 1 hour.
Turn off heat, open oven door slightly, and leave cake in oven for1 hour longer.

Let cool to room temperature.
Refrigerate 4 hours or overnight.

Serves: 16

This cheesecake seems to always disappear quickly.

Pineapple Mandarin Orange Cake

Jeanine Merritt

Cake:

1 box butter yellow cake
½ cup oil
4 eggs
Small can mandarin oranges (with juice)

Frosting:

Large can crushed pineapple (with juice)
1 small package vanilla instant pudding
8 ounce Cool Whip

Pre-heat oven to 350° F.

Mix cake as directed on box, but with oil, 4 eggs and mandarin oranges, undrained.
Pour batter evenly into three, 9-inch, greased and floured cake pans.

Bake @ 350° F. for 20-23 minutes until toothpick comes out clean when inserted into cake.
Allow cake to cool on racks.

Frost:

Mix together crushed pineapple and vanilla pudding.
Fold in Cool Whip. Frost cake.

Note - Pineapple Mandarin Orange Cake is really moist and is one of Jeanine's most frequently requested cake recipes. This cake is usually served for the family's birthday celebrations. Everybody likes it!

Mint Chocolate Fudge

Jareth Hammond

2¾ cups sugar
4-ounces unsweetened chocolate
3 tablespoons butter, plus more for greasing pan
1 cup half-and-half
1 tablespoon corn syrup
1½ tablespoon peppermint extract

Grease an 8x8-inch pan with butter.

In a heavy-bottomed saucepan, combine sugar, chocolate, 1½ tablespoons of the butter, half-and-half and corn syrup.
Over medium heat, stir with a wooden spoon until sugar is dissolved and chocolate is melted.
Increase heat and bring to a boil.
Reduce heat to medium-low, cover and boil for 3 min.
Remove cover and attach a candy thermometer to the pot.
Cook until the thermometer reads 234° F.
Remove from heat and add remaining butter. Do not stir.
Let mixture cool 10 min. or until temperature drops to 130° F.
Add peppermint and mix until well-blended and the shiny texture becomes matte.

Pour into the prepared pan. Let sit in cool, dry area until firm.
Cut into 2-inch pieces.

Yield: 30 pieces

Rice Pudding

Jareth Hammond

1 cup white rice, uncooked
1 cup water
4 cups milk
4 tablespoons butter
¾ cup sugar
½ teaspoon ginger
½ teaspoon nutmeg
¼ teaspoon cloves
1½ teaspoon cinnamon
1 egg
1 teaspoon vanilla

In medium saucepan, combine rice, water, 1 cup milk, and 2 tablespoons butter; heat until boiling. Cover. Reduce heat to simmer. Cook for 15-20 minutes or until rice is tender.

In separate saucepan, combine remaining milk, butter, sugar, ginger, nutmeg, cloves and cinnamon. Heat to a light boil.

In small mixing bowl, beat the egg and add 1 cup of the milk mixture. Mix until fully incorporated. Add egg mixture to milk mixture. Cook until thickened slightly.

Add cooked rice and vanilla. Cook for 5-10 minutes. Remove from heat and set aside to cool. Mixture will thicken as it stands.

May serve chilled or at room temperature.
Serves: 4-6

Baklava
Jareth Hammond

1 cup sugar
1 cup honey
¾ cup water
1 tablespoon lemon juice
2 cinnamon sticks
2 (1-inch) strips lemon zest
2 pinches ground cloves
3 pinches ground cardamom
1¼ lb walnuts
2 teaspoons ground cinnamon
¼ teaspoon salt
2 sticks unsalted butter
1 lb phyllo, thawed according to package instructions

Syrup:
In medium saucepan: combine sugar, honey, water, lemon juice, cinnamon sticks, lemon zest, cloves and cardamom.
Cook over medium heat, stirring occasionally, until sugar is dissolved. Reduce heat to medium-low.
Cook until syrup is slightly thickened, about 10 minutes.

Filling and Dough:
Using a sharp knife or food processor, finely chop walnuts.
In mixing bowl, combine walnuts, cinnamon and salt.
Stir well to combine.
In small saucepan, melt butter over low heat.
Using a pastry brush, lightly coat a 9x13 or 10x15-inch baking dish with some of the melted butter.

Open the package of phyllo and lay the thin sheets on a clean work surface next to your baking dish.
If the sheets measure approximately the same size, proceed from here. If they are larger, use a sharp knife to cut the phyllo sheets

approximately the same size as your baking dish. Discard any scraps.
Cover the sheets with a lightly damp kitchen towel, as the sheets of phyllo dry out very quickly, if left uncovered.

Pre-heat oven to 350° F.

Place two of the sheets of phyllo in the bottom of the buttered baking dish and lightly brush top with melted butter.

Repeat this procedure with 7 more sheets of phyllo, for a total of 8 layers.

Spread a layer of the nut mixture evenly over the buttered phyllo sheets. Repeat with 8 more sheets of phyllo, buttering every other layer as before, and top these sheets with another
layer of the nut mixture.

Continue this layering process, buttering sheets of phyllo and topping each 8 sheets with a layer of nuts, until you have used all the nut mixture.

Layer any remaining sheets of phyllo on top, buttering between every other layer, until all sheets have been used.

Use a sharp knife to make four lengthwise cuts through the layered phyllo at 1½-inch increments to form diamond shapes. You should have 5 (1½-inch wide) strips lengthwise.
Then cut diagonally at 1½-inch increments to form diamond shapes. You should end up with 35-40 diamond-shaped pieces of baklava.

Bake the baklava until golden brown, about 40 minutes.

Remove from oven, set aside on a wire rack to cool 10 min.
Remove cinnamon sticks and lemon zest from syrup.

Using a ladle or small measuring cup, drizzle the cooled syrup over the warm baklava.

Allow to stand several hours before serving. Yield: 35-40

Chocolate Coated Toffee Pieces
Jareth Hammond

1 1/3 cups sugar
1 cup butter, melted
3 Tablespoons water
1 Tablespoon light corn syrup
2 16-ounce Pkgs. Semi-Sweet chocolate chips
1 cup slivered almonds

Place a sheet of parchment paper over a cookie sheet and set aside.
In medium saucepan, combine sugar, butter, water and corn syrup.
Cook over medium heat, stirring occasionally, until candy thermometer reads 300° F.
Remove from heat and let mixture settle for 15 seconds.
Pour toffee mixture onto prepared cookie sheet.
Using an offset spatula, spread to ¼-inch thickness.
Set aside until toffee has cooled and hardened, then break into medium sized pieces.
In a double boiler, melt 2/3 of the chocolate over hot, (but not

simmering) water that is not touching the bottom of the container holding the chocolate.
Melt the chocolate until it reaches a temperature of 110° F.
Remove the top of the double boiler containing the chocolate and place it on a towel on the counter.
Beat in the remaining 1/3 of chocolate, letting the mixture cool to 87° F. Mixture should be smooth and glossy.

Hold at that temperature by moving the container on and off the hot water.
Dip toffee pieces into tempered chocolate. Top with almonds.
Set aside until chocolate has set.

Yield: 35-50 Medium-sized pieces

Jareth brought this delicious candy to us for a "taste test."
This recipe passed with flying colors.

These chocolate-coated pieces have an authentic, high-end toffee flavor and consistency, along with a nice *crunch* that good toffee is famous for.

Jareth Hammond is on his way to becoming a noted chef.
He constantly works on new creations and meticulously refines his original recipes in his personal kitchen.

Jareth's goal is to attend cooking school, and after graduating, offer his distinctively different culinary talents to the world.

Congratulations, Jareth... and good luck to this future chef.

Melissa's Party Pumpkin Torte

Mayers Jewelry /Jewelry Designers & Emporium
Melissa Mayer

Crust:

24 crushed Graham Crackers (approx. 2 cups)
½ teaspoon cinnamon
½ cup sugar
½ cup butter

Mix ingredients together and press into a 9x13-inch pan to form crust.

Second layer:

2 eggs, beaten
½ cup sugar
1 (8-oz) package cream cheese, softened

Mix all ingredients well. Pour over Graham Cracker crust.

Bake @ 350° F. for 20 minutes.

Filling:
2 cups pumpkin
3 eggs, separated
½ cup sugar
½ cup milk
¼ teaspoon salt
1 teaspoon cinnamon
1 envelope plain gelatin
½ cup sugar

In saucepan, cook pumpkin, egg yolks, ½ cup sugar, milk, salt, and cinnamon, until ingredients have thickened.

Remove from heat.

Soak gelatin in ¼ cup cold water, then add to the above filling ingredients.
Allow to cool.

Beat egg whites until stiffened.
Add ½ cup sugar. Fold into pumpkin mixture.
Pour over cream cheese layer.

Refrigerate Torte until ready to serve.

Top with a spoonful of whipped cream.
Sprinkle with dash of cinnamon to garnish.

Note - Max says that this recipe is really good. He enjoys this Pumpkin Torte every time Melissa makes it.

Great served at a party or a family gathering.

Hahn's Blonde Brownies
James R. Hahn

1 (1-lb) box light brown sugar
4 eggs
2 cups Biscuit Mix
½ cup white chocolate chip morsels
2 cups chopped pecans

Mix together light brown sugar, eggs and Biscuit Mix.
Stir in pecans. Pour into a greased 9x13-inch baking dish.
Bake @ 350° F for 35 minutes.
Cool and cut into squares for serving.

Note - My husband is partial to blondes.

Lightning Fast Key Lime Pie
Randy Johnson

1 (8-ounce) container Whipped topping
1 can condensed milk
½ cup lime juice
1 graham cracker pie crust

Blend whipped topping, condensed milk and lime juice together until very smooth.
Pour into graham cracker pie crust.

Refrigerate for approximately 1-2 hours before you are ready to serve.

Note - This is possibly the easiest Key Lime Pie recipe ever, ergo the name...Lightning Fast.

Dublin Pecan Pie
Dot Hahn

1 cup sugar
½ cup corn syrup
¼ cup butter, melted
3 eggs, well beaten
1 cup pecans
Dash of salt
¾ teaspoon vanilla

1 unbaked 9-inch pie crust

Pre-heat oven to 350° F.

Mix sugar, syrup and butter.
Add other ingredients.
Pour into unbaked pie crust.
Lower oven heat to 325° F.

Bake 50-60 minutes or until pie is set.

Note - For over a decade, Dot lived in Dublin, Georgia.
She baked many of these delicious pies while there, using pecans she gathered from trees surrounding her family's home.

Ice Cream Pie

Dot Hahn

1 package Nestle's Chocolate Chips
1 stick butter or margarine
1 cup Rice Krispies
Vanilla Ice Cream /or Ice Milk

Melt together chocolate chips and butter.
Reserve about 2 tablespoons to drizzle over top of pie.
Add Rice Krispies and mix well.
(This forms the pie crust.)
Refrigerate just long enough to make mixture pliable.
Press and mold this mixture into a round/or rectangular pie plate to make the crust.
(If mixture gets too hard to mold, thaw briefly at room temperature.)
Fill shell with softened ice cream.
Cover with foil and freeze.

Note - If using a round pan, slice like pie.
If using a rectangular pan, cut into squares like brownies.

Use a fork as you eat this...it is brittle...but GOOD.

For a delicious, but healthier alternative, use Frozen Yogurt.

Try assorted flavors of ice cream or yogurt to make this different each time you serve it.

Sweet Potato Soufflé

Dot Hahn

2 cups sweet potatoes
(Dot bakes about 3 potatoes for this recipe/or uses
2 cans of # 2 size)

1¼ cups sugar
2 eggs
¾ stick butter
1 cup milk
½ teaspoon cinnamon
½ teaspoon nutmeg

Cook and mash potatoes. Or use canned.
Add all remaining ingredients, mix well.
Pour into a 2-quart casserole.
Bake @ 400° F for 20 minutes.
Remove from oven.
Spread topping evenly over top of casserole.

Topping:
¾ cup crushed cornflakes
½ cup brown sugar
½ cup pecans
¾ stick butter

Mix together butter and brown sugar.
Add pecans and corn flakes
Spread over top of soufflé

Note - Use frosted flakes for a sweeter topping ... They're Great!

Sour Cream Coconut Cake

Dot Hahn

Cake:
1 box Deluxe Yellow cake mix

Icing Ingredients:
2 cups sour cream
2 cups powdered sugar
2 packages frozen coconut (6-oz. size)

Icing preparation:
Mix sour cream, coconut and powdered sugar.
Place in refrigerator...Let stand overnight.

Follow the package directions on the cake mix and bake as instructed.
Allow layers to cool.
Slice layers in half to make four layers.

When ready to frost cake, remove icing from refrigerator.
Spread icing over cake layers.
Cover cake and refrigerate overnight.

Note - Cake is better if left in refrigerator for at least 2 days. This is Dot's favorite coconut cake. You would never believe it is made from a mix.

Beverages

Sparkling Party Punch

Donna James

½ gallon ginger ale
Red seedless grapes
Sparkling white grape juice, chilled

Make an ice ring of ginger ale and red grapes.

***To make ice ring*:**
Pour ginger ale into a tube or bundt pan and sprinkle in red grapes to decorate.
Freeze.

When ready to serve, place ice ring in punch bowl.
Pour in sparkling grape juice.

Note - This punch not only makes a nice presentation, but the floating ice ring keeps the punch cold for hours.

Tropical Punch

Donna James

1 large 46-ounce can pineapple juice
1 large 46-ounce can apricot nectar
3 cans (6-oz) limeade-concentrate, thawed
3 quarts Ginger Ale, chilled

Combine the first three ingredients.
Refrigerate to chill.
When ready to serve, add Ginger Ale.

Note- This is a great tasting non-alcoholic punch that all ages can enjoy.

Mocha-Latte Punch

Steve M.

4 cups brewed coffee
¼ sugar (more/less to taste)
4 cups milk
4 cups Chocolate Ice Cream, softened

Combine coffee and sugar. Stir until sugar is completely dissolved. Refrigerate 2 hours.

To serve:
Pour into a punch bowl.
Add milk and blend well.
Top with a scoop of Chocolate Ice Cream.
Stir until blended.

Orange Dream Smoothie

Steve M.

1¾ cup milk
½ pint Vanilla Ice Cream
1/3 cup frozen orange juice concentrate
1 tablespoon non-dairy creamer

Put all ingredients into a blender.
Blend until smooth.

Note - Try adding other fruit such as pineapple, bananas, strawberries, or kiwi to the mixture.

This is a great way to get your daily serving of fruit.

Banana-Split Smoothie

Bill Freeman

2 ripe Bananas
3 cups milk
1 package (10-oz) frozen sweetened strawberries, thawed
1½ pint Chocolate Ice Cream, divided

In blender:
Blend bananas.
Add milk, strawberries, and ½ pint of the ice cream.
Blend until smooth and creamy.

Pour smoothie into tall soda glasses.
Top with scoop of Chocolate Ice Cream.

Note - Add Cool Whip and a Cherry on Top ... just like a real Banana Split.

Kahlua Ice Cream Smoothie

Marion Mitchell

1 cup Kahlua
1 pint Vanilla Ice Cream
1 cup half-and-half
¼ teaspoon almond or vanilla extract

Combine all ingredients in blender.
Add 1 heaping cup of ice cubes.
Blend until smooth and frothy.

Delicious.

Strawberry Banana Smoothie

Chuck Stinson

2 bananas, sliced
1 pint strawberries, quartered
1 carton (8-ounce) strawberry yogurt
¼ cup orange juice
Sugar or sweetener to taste (optional)

In blender:
Blend together all ingredients until rich and smooth.
Serve immediately.

Tropical Fruit Smoothie

Chuck Stinson

2 containers (8-ounce) vanilla yogurt
1 cup frozen blueberries
1 cup frozen peach slices
1 (8-ounce) can pineapple chucks, drained

Process all ingredients in blender.
Scrape down sides of blender to mix.

Blend until smooth and fruity.

Note - This is a recipe where you can get as creative as you wish to be. Experiment with strawberries, bananas, mixed berries, etc.

Whiskey Sour Slush
Julie Freeman

1 can frozen Orange Juice concentrate
1 can frozen Lemonade concentrate
6 cans water (using juice cans)
2 cups strong Black Tea (4 tea bags to 1 qt. water)
1 750 ml bottle of whiskey

Boil tea bags in 1 quart of water and let steep to enhance flavor. While tea is still hot, mix in orange juice and lemonade concentrate. Add 6 cans of water, using empty juice cans to measure. Pour in contents of full bottle of whiskey. Stir to blend.

Pour mixture into a suitable container and freeze for 2 days. (It takes 2 days to freeze because of the alcohol content.) *Stir from time to time during freezing process to keep ingredients from separating.*

To Serve: Use ice cream scoop to fill glass with a scoop of icy slush. Fill glass with Lemon-Lime soda. Garnish with lemon or orange slices. Top with a Cherry.

Serve and Enjoy!

Note - Julie said this recipe was handed down from "friend to friend" at "party after party." This drink is good served at a Wine & Cheese event, House-Warming, or Any Excuse to Party.

We tried this one. It's great. Thanks, Julie!

Tequiza-Rita
C. Moon

2 (12-oz) bottles of Tequiza brand beer, chilled
½ cup chilled Patron tequila
½ cup limeade concentrate, thawed
1 lime, cut into 8 wedges
¼ cup Margarita salt
Ice cubes

Rub 4 lime wedges around the rims of 4 Margarita glasses. Turn glasses upside down and dip rims into salt to coat.

In pitcher:
Combine Tequiza beer, Patron tequila and limeade.

Fill prepared/salted Margarita glasses with ice cubes.

Pour Tequiza-Rita into glasses and garnish with the 4 remaining lime wedges.

Drink immediately... and enjoy!

Serves: 4

Note - You can use any beer of your choice, but Tequiza Beer is especially good for this drink, as it has a nice lime flavor and compliments the limeade and tequila.

Fiesta Sangria Punch

C. Moon

4 cups white wine
1/3 cup Patron Citronge
¼ cup triple sec
2 sliced oranges
2 sliced limes
2 sliced lemons
1 large can fruit cocktail
1 liter bottle Ginger Ale

Combine all ingredients except Ginger Ale.
Cover mixture and refrigerate at least 3-4 hours.

When ready to serve:

Pour Sangria mixture into a
decorative punch bowl.

Add Ginger Ale and stir to mix.

Serve immediately. **Do not drive!**

Gag
Foods

Recipe for Main Street Flavors

1 Small Downtown Main Street
2 Heaping Handfuls of Colorful Characters
Gales of Laughter
A Pinch of Sarcasm
Loads of Special Sauce.
4 Letter Words
Dash of Cayenne pepper (for the Hot and Spicy Version)

Start with one small downtown Main Street.
Combine a local blend of Colorful Characters.
Throw in a pinch of Sarcasm.
Add Special Sauce, both Sweet and Sour.
Sprinkle in 4 Letter Words. (entirely optional)

Toss together until completely "Mixed Up."
Pepper to taste for Hot and Spicy Version.

Blend until you have the perfect consistency for Main Street Flavors.

Bake in a sweltering 90°-100° Summer Heat.
Follow instructions for cooking at Higher Altitudes.*

**Due to living "On the Ridge" at a whopping 200-plus feet above sea level in Central Florida.*

Lisa's Famous Microwave Popcorn

Lisa Pederson
Gallery and Frame Shop

Ingredients: Publix brand Movie Theater Butter
(Lisa's choice... feel free to use your own personal favorite.)

Remove the outer plastic wrapper.
Place in microwave with appropriate side up. (This is marked on the bag.)
Most newer microwaves have a popcorn setting. If yours does not have this option, start with 3½ minutes.
You may have to adjust cooking time depending on your oven.
Be warned! Not all kernels will pop.
When popping is complete, carefully remove bag from the oven.
Caution! It will be very hot.
Pull apart the top of the bag by pulling opposite corners of the bag in a diagonal direction to prevent steam from burning your hands.
Salt and butter are already in the bag, but you may add more to taste.

To impress your guests, you may choose a decorative bowl for serving.

Note- Lisa suggests keeping the popcorn in the original bag. This works best because you can rub the kernels against the side of the bag to get more butter and salt on each bite.

Serving suggestions:
Best if served with Coca-Cola or other carbonated beverage.

Lisa says: "This is a good vegetarian meal...corn is a vegetable".

Cheese Crackers with Peanut Butter

Lisa Pederson
The Gallery and Frame Shop

For a fast meal, Lisa recommends:
Cheese Crackers with Peanut Butter.

Several brands are very good, but Lisa's favorites are Austin or Lance.

Instructions:
Tear plastic wrapper.
Remove each cracker separately as you eat them.
This keeps crackers contained so that you may perform other tasks as you eat.

Serving suggestion:
Best served with Coca-Cola or other carbonated beverage.

Note - Cheese Crackers with Peanut Butter Provides the following nutritious ingredients:

Protein [from Peanut Butter]
Cereal [from Crackers]
Dairy [from Cheese]

<u>Ron's Armadinna</u>

Humane Society of Polk County
Lisa Baker - Exec. Director

1 freshly found Armadillo
Salt
Pepper
Onions
Green Peppers
Garlic

You will need a 2-inch white oak board, sand paper, and aluminum foil. Obtain a freshly killed armadillo (usually in the right lane; armadillos don't normally make it to the middle of the road.) Split the armadillo (if not already split by the tire) down the middle. Place armadillo, shell side up, on a freshly sanded, 2-inch thick, white oak board. Season generously with ½ lb of salt and a cup of pepper. Cover with onions, garlic, and green peppers.

Wrap in foil and place in 350° oven for about half a day.
Don't ever plan to use this oven again...*<u>Ever!</u>*
Remove from oven and remove foil. Throw away the armadillo and what is left of the onions, garlic and peppers, and serve the oak board. An electric chainsaw should be used to carve the dish.

Serve with: Any color wine, as long as it has a screw-off cap.
Serves: A family of 10.

Will keep in the refrigerator for months. Good heated up on cold winter nights when you need something light. Bon appetit.

This recipe is an Erison family tradition passed down for generations; even as far back to the Viking explorers.
Yes ... even then the armadillo was a pest.

Ericson's Elephant Stew

Ron Ericson

1 medium sized Elephant
2 Rabbits (Optional)*
Salt
Pepper

Cut the elephant into small, bite size pieces.

Add enough brown gravy to completely cover.

Cook elephant over kerosene fire for about 4 weeks, at approximately 462° F.

This recipe will serve 3,600 hungry people.

** If more company is expected, the 2 rabbits may be added; but do this only in an emergency... Most people do not like hare in their stew.*

Black-Eyed Please

James R. Hahn

Ritz crackers
Cream cheese, softened
Pepper
Sliced bread-and-butter pickles
Black Olives

In order of ingredients, start stacking.

Spread softened cream cheese on Ritz Cracker.
Dash of pepper on top of the cream cheese.

Center pickle on cracker.
Add black olive for center of Black Eye.

(Add a shot of hot sauce for the "bloodshot" version)

Note - This is a fun party food. It will get conversation started. Place on serving platter. Have fun at your next event.

Here's looking at you!

Main Street Merchants & Supporters

Arcade Coffee & Sandwich Shoppe
Curt and Terry Koch

If you are fortunate enough to be downtown in historic Lake Wales, and want to experience something refreshingly different, stop in and visit this great little place.

Curt and Terry are prime examples of how *not* to judge a book by its cover. The Coffee Shoppe is right across the hall from our art gallery. For the first few days, as my husband and I were moving our original paintings into the gallery, Curt would stare, stone-faced at us, while playing the theme song from *"The Twilight Zone"* on his left-handed guitar. Talk about first impressions! We later came to the realization that Curt is quite harmless. We even found a soft, chewy center, beneath his hard and crusty, outer shell. But he really had us going there for the first week or so into our new venture. So if you think you can judge a book by its cover...Read On.

The Arcade Coffee & Sandwich Shoppe has an extensive menu which includes a full breakfast. Then there's the infamous *Rembrandt Wrap,* a hot and spicy egg salad concoction. (see recipe). For lunch, be sure to try a New York Deli-style Rueben sandwich and/or Hot Pastrami on Rye, using only the finest Boar's Head products. (No nasty preservatives, Yeah.) Other mouth-watering favorites include freshly made chicken and tuna salads and wraps. It's all good; I've tried it all.

Quench your thirst with a Tropical fruit Smoothie, or enjoy iced or hot coffee specials made from rich, aromatic coffees imported from all over the world. (My favorite is Costa Rican.)

Freshness is assured, as the owners arrive at 5:30 a.m. to start food preparation. Coffee makers are set to brew hot, steaming java when the first sleepy-eyed customers make their way down the sidewalk and through the doors of the Arcade Coffee & Sandwich Shoppe. The interior is rustic and natural, with a woodland-forest motif. Interesting artifacts abound, including a hand-made mahogany and cedar canoe, built by Martin Two Feathers.

Upon entering the establishment, you will be greeted by Terry, (the Sweet & Pretty one) who will carefully take your order and then pass it over to Curt, (well, you know) who cooks, creates and meticulously embellishes the dishes...Who knew?

Enjoy your meal in the breezeway of the historic Arcade building or dine *al fresco* at the sidewalk café out front. If you're lucky, you may hear that infamous *theme song* being played as background music to enhance your dining experience. This is the best place in town to catch up on the latest gossip. Bring your laptop to surf the net, via wireless connection, provided by the Coffee Shoppe. (CUSTOMERS ONLY-per Curt.)

Located in the Rhodesbilt Arcade at 229 E. Stuart Ave.
Phone 863-676-8510

Chalet Suzanne®
Restaurant and Inn

3800 Chalet Suzanne Drive
Lake Wales FL 33859

Just on the outskirts of Downtown Lake Wales you will find the enchanting Chalet Suzanne Country Inn & Restaurant. This historic landmark has been in the Hinshaw family since 1931 when Carl and Bertha Hinshaw, Sr. created the Inn and named it after their only daughter, Suzanne. Four generations of the Hinshaw family have lived and worked on this beautiful estate, and have dedicated themselves to the family tradition of excellence. Many well-known celebrities have visited the Chalet. It is proudly listed on the National Register of Historic Places. The Inn, nestled on a 100-acre estate, has 30 lovely rooms, each one unique, and delightfully different.

Whether you drive your car to Chalet Suzanne, or fly your plane in on its 2500 ft. private airstrip, you will be made to feel welcome and relaxed in your *"home away from home."* For hungry diners, food is served in five quaint rooms overlooking the lake. These rooms are tastefully appointed with antiques and stained glass. Every corner glows with vintage lamps from far away places.
Chalet Suzanne's award-winning restaurant is listed by Duncan Hines in his leisure travel book Adventures in Good Eating. Chalet Suzanne was selected by Uncle Ben's Rice_as one of the10 Best Country Inns. The restaurant was named to Florida Trend Magazine's *Golden Spoon Award* "Hall of Fame." Other awards include Travel/Holiday *Fine Dining Award* and Florida Monthly Magazine *Best of Florida* and *Best Bed & Breakfast.* Gourmet Magazine calls Chalet Suzanne's cuisine-food... *"Glorious"* While on the grounds, visit the Inn's Soup Cannery. After over 40 years of production, these recipes have been served in many noteworthy places, including the Governor's Mansion, Worlds Fair, and on TWA and Eastern Airlines international flights. Thanks to Lunar Module pilot, *James B. Irwin,* the soup was selected by NASA to be aboard Apollo 15 in its 1973 trip to the Moon. The soup went back into space on Apollo 16.

Romaineâ, the signature soup, is served with every meal at the restaurant and can be found with a special label, known as Moon Soupâ. Thirteen unique gourmet soups, and three sauces that were developed by Carl Hinshaw, are processed for gift-giving all over the globe. Explore the Gift Boutique, Museum, Ceramic Salon, Vineyard, Autograph Garden, and Courtyard Spa. If what you've read about this history is intriguing...and you agree that Chalet Suzanne Restaurant and County Inn is really a special place to visit, try spending a little time there. Stay in this quiet oasis, amidst the excitement of the many Central Florida attractions, and become part of the proud heritage of the Hinshaw family.

Phone 863-676-6011 or 800-433-6011

www.chaletsuzanne.com
email - info@chaletsuzanne.com

Rick DePalma
Coldwell Banker Ridge Properties

Rick DePalma is a dedicated real estate professional and devoted friend. Rick specializes in residential, condo, and waterfront properties, but also handles all other aspects of real estate. Rick is the kind of guy who never seems to meet a stranger. His clients feel the same way about him. Rick is never too busy to answer his phone, or to talk to a client about a real estate investment. In today's, fast-paced world, it is rare to experience the personal touch, so necessary, for relationship-building. Rick puts himself into his client's shoes, and goes the extra mile. This *client first* attitude, has put Rick DePalma, at the top of his game.

Rick's office is located in the historic district, just a few doors down from the Rhodesbilt Arcade, at 247 E Stuart Avenue. Rick loves the combination of the rich history of Downtown, Lake Wales, along with the camaraderie of his friends and fellow merchants. Rick is, as the song says... A well respected man about town. When not working with clients, Rick's true passion is the time he shares with his wife, Julia. If you are thinking about making a move to Lake Wales or the surrounding area, give him a call. With Rick DePalma on your side, your move is sure to be a smooth transition.

For more information: Call Rick on his cell phone @ 863-605-0414 or visit his website at www.homesinlakewales.com

The Lake Wales Downtown Times
Todd and Lisa Hammond

This monthly publication is where you will "Get the Scoop" on all the happening events in Downtown Lake Wales. *Downtown Times* is locally owned and operated by Todd and Lisa Hammond, who also serve as editor and publisher. There is always something happening downtown, with its wonderful and unique shops.

There is not one chain store or Big Box among them. Inside the pages, you will find the *Downtown Directory*, listing retail shops and galleries, restaurants, services, and visitor information. Also, check out the *Calendar of Events* so you won't miss a thing.

Out-of-town visitors can have *Downtown Times* mailed to their home or business for just $16.95 a year. You can live vicariously through the locals in *"Sunny Florida"* while supporting the area economy and the Historic Downtown District.

I wanted to take this opportunity to thank Todd and Lisa. *Downtown Times* was the very first publication to announce this book when it was still very much a concept...Thanks, Todd & Lisa.

For more information/or to subscribe:

Moondragon Media Group
229 E. Stuart Avenue, Suite 10
Lake Wales FL 33853

Phone 863-676-2004
email: moondragonmediagroup@msn.com

<u>The Gallery and Frame Shop</u>

Lisa Pederson - owner

249 E. Stuart Avenue
863-676-2821

Lisa Pederson is a Florida native; born and raised in Lake Wales. She graduated from Lake Wales High School and the University of Florida.

After working in Orlando, she returned to Lake Wales when she purchased *The Gallery and Frame Shop* in 1988.
Lisa has been framing artwork and other treasures ever since.

To Lisa Pederson...*Cook* is a four letter word.
Those of you who know her are probably wondering...
"Why on earth would Lisa be featured in a cookbook?"
The answer is simple. *Lisa can cook, she chooses not to.*

In Lisa's defense, she says, and I quote "I do have to eat...and since necessity is the mother of invention, I have adapted."

Lisa has a couple of great recipes she shares with you in this book. Real recipes that she learned from her mother and grandmother. These delicious meals have been a part of Lisa's diet, and a staple on her table, for as long as she remembers.

Both, Creole Steak and Scalloped Salmon, are family recipes. After serving these fast and fabulous dishes for her dinner guests, Lisa has often had very good cooks ask her for the recipes. Her guests were as surprised as Lisa!

Lisa would be the first one to admit that she is not a cook.
But notice how creative she gets with serving suggestions, and her presentations skills are nothing short of divine. Lisa never underestimate the impact of colorful serving platters and decorative bowls. (See Lisa's Microwave Popcorn.)

What Lisa really excels at is her uncanny ability to rationalize and/or justify that her concoctions are even meals at all. She can really sell you on this concept and will make a believer out of you.

The blinders are off. I will never see Cheese crackers the same way again.

Lisa Pederson knows how to have fun and is a colorful addition to Stuart Avenue. Watch her strut her stuff as a participant in the annual Mardi-Gras festivities, where she literally, "kicks up her heels," along the parade route.

Lisa brings her own, unique brand of Main Street Flavor
to downtown Lake Wales.

To find out more about The Gallery and Frame Shop visit

www.thegalleryandframeshop.com

Gary L. Bear Barber & Style Shop

Gary Bear

If downtown Lake Wales was Mayberry RFD, then Gary Bear would be our *Floyd*, the barber. For over 47 years, Gary Bear has been a vital part of the historic district. Gary has seen three generations come and go through the door of his Barber Shop. His original clients now have children and grandchildren who enter his shop, shaggy and unshaved, and exit, well-groomed and coiffed.

It is a pleasure just to be in the same company as Gary Bear. He has an infectious laugh...one so contagious, that you find yourself smiling, before you even know what is so funny. Few people have this ability; Gary is a master of it.
Gary and his wife, Pam, have observed many changes to downtown Lake Wales. They have witnessed this trans-formation through the

same front window of Gary's barber shop. While outwardly, the town has changed, the inside of the shop, for the most part, has remained the same. You know you have arrived, when you see the revolving barber pole, located just outside Gary's front door. Duck inside for a shave or a haircut, and sit down in a barber chair, steeped in local history. Gary will have you looking stylish, in a flash, and you will leave the barber shop with a big smile on your face ... guaranteed.

Gary L. Bear Barber & Style Shop
203 E Stuart Avenue
863-676-2104

James R. Hahn Productions

James R. Hahn - Artist
229 E Stuart Avenue Suite 15
Lake Wales, FL 33853

Strategically located, front and center, in the historic Rhodesbilt Arcade building, is the art gallery and working studio of James R. Hahn. The fusion of art and history came together like hand-in-glove, when Hahn opened his art gallery in the historic district. The merger has become a true, symbiotic relationship between the artist and the city of Lake Wales.

As a native Floridian, the artist has an intrinsic appreciation of Florida's natural settings. His treatment of waves, and the movement of light on water, has placed James R. Hahn as a fore-runner in marine art. While in college, working toward his art degree, Hahn was chosen to paint the original mural for the Cabbage Patch Kids. With over 30 years experience, Hahn's artistic talents are in constant demand. Hahn, a world traveler, has visited numerous ports-of-call. One of his most memorable destinations includes Lake Louise in Banff Canada, where he was originally inspired to paint. Hahn was also awe-struck by the art and architecture of Florence, Italy and with the myriad canals and waterways of Venice. These magnificent landmarks are featured themes in his work.

Hahn's work eventually lead him to Central America. After living and working for one year in Costa Rica, he returned to South Florida where he opened James R. Hahn Productions in Vero Beach, FL. Hahn splits his time between the two cities when he is not working *on location*, for a specific project. After an exhaustive work schedule, Hahn relishes the peace and tranquility that the "downtown scene" offers. Hahn has designed and created large-scale murals for his private and celebrity clients. One of his most recent works is an original mural 80 ft. long and 20 ft. tall. This large painting depicts tropical gardens and features a summer cottage in the foreground. The painted cottage was a creative way for Hahn to incorporate existing windows that are a structural part of the building's façade. This eye-catching mural has helped reshape the face of historic downtown.

Hahn is often quoted as saying, *"We help our clients see the Big Picture."* This statement relates to the fact that he provides his clients, large works of original art, while at the same time giving them the "*wow*" factor. To view a few of Hahn's murals, just visit Mr. Manatee's Casual Grille in Vero Beach, or the Platinum Club in the Sunrise FL, Bank Atlantic Center. Hahn recently was selected to create a work, that was exhibited & sold at the Salvador Dali Museum in St. Petersburg, Florida. If you visit Lake Wales or Vero Beach, you may spot the artist working on an original painting in one of his studios. The galleries have a collection of Giclee and limited edition prints, including *Hahn-highlighted*, unique-variation prints on canvas.

For an extensive overview of Hahn's artistic repertoire, visit his website: www.jamesrhahn.com or phone: 772-713-9703.
Gallery hours: Lake Wales/Vero Beach...are by appointment.

Hidden Gardens Bed & Breakfast

Harold and Jessica Bray

Located on picturesque Lake Wailes, and within walking distance of historic downtown, is Hidden Gardens Bed & Breakfast. Built in 1913, in traditional Key West style, the house exudes a tranquil, Florida charm.

Four guest rooms are located on the upper level and stand ready to accommodate even the most weary traveler. After a great sleep, wake up to the aroma of morning coffee and a delicious home-cooked breakfast. As its name implies, Hidden Gardens has lush, tropical landscaping. A crystal-clear swimming pool, private sauna, and tea house, are located on the grounds for the enjoyment of each guest.

Winding paths lead you to unexpected treasures around each bend. Wander around and you will discover a secluded Zen Garden, hidden behind a wall of bamboo. Find a bench, relax and meditate, as you listen to the sound of the wind through the palm trees.

Smell the intoxicating scent of orange blossoms, and remember, just in case you forgot, that you are in Central Florida. Take a leisurely stroll around the historic district and experience the rich heritage of Lake Wales. Harold and Jessica searched for just the right community to open Tres Jolie and Hidden Gardens Bed & Breakfast; and after a visit to Lake Wales, the couple found their new home. The Brays are excited to be part of such a rich and robust community, and we are certainly glad they are here.

Hidden Gardens Bed & Breakfast
33 North Lakeshore Blvd.
Lake Wales, FL 33853

For booking info: 863-676-4470

Mayer Jewelers

Jewelry Designers & Emporium
Max & Melissa Mayer

Mayer Jewelers has been family owned and operated for over 34 years and has a prominent place in historic downtown.
Located on E. Stuart Avenue, Mayer Jewelers has a long tradition of giving exceptional service to its many loyal customers.

Max and Melissa enjoy the history of the local area, and have seen a lot of changes during their time as downtown merchants. Max is also a visionary, and sees the expected growth of the county to continue to bring new visitors to our exciting, historic district.

Max Mayer is an accomplished jewelry designer who creates custom, one-of-a-kind pieces for his discriminating clientele.
If you choose, Max can work with your existing gold or diamonds to create a totally new, and distinctively different, work of wearable art.

Diamonds are a specialty at Mayer Jewelers. Max will painstakingly create a stunning new ring or pendant from a diamond that you already own. Or, you can choose a new diamond from a large selection of modern or vintage rings.

Mayer Jewelers & Emporium carries antique and estate jewelry, sterling silver flatware and accessories, and a selection of pocket watches. For the discerning connoisseur, there is the ever-fashionable, Rolex.

Mayer Jewelers is located at 201 E. Stuart Avenue
Lake Wales, Florida 33853 call: 863-676-1317

Architectural Drafting & Residential Design

Mel Percy P.B.D.

Mel's office space is a good indicator of his creative talent and unique sense of style. The walls of Mel's downtown office display his Native American heritage. Peace pipes, a Talking stick, a 7-ft. Totem pole, and many other Native American treasures adorn the space. His most recent art acquisition is the painting ***Jealousy of the Malcontents***, by James R. Hahn, that was on exhibit at the Salvador Dali Museum.

MP Architectural Drafting & Residential Design is located in a remodeled and completely renovated building, listed on the National Register of Historic Places. Mel specializes in building design, site plans, construction document preparation, and permit application assistance. Mel is an avid fan of the architecture of Frank Lloyd Wright.

Mel's wife, Maria, works with him in their downtown office. They *"come out to play"* on special event nights such as Bike Night. Mel's passion is riding his Harley-Davidson and feeling the wind in his hair. When bikers gather downtown for this special event, you will hear the roar of Mel's Harley as he and Maria cruise into town. Their relationship is a cultural melting pot. Maria was born in Santander, in northern Spain. Her fiery and passionate personality is in direct contrast to Mel's introspective and analytical approach to life. Together, this couple cook up a double dose of ... Main Street Flavors.

Architectural Drafting & Residential Design
254 E Stuart Ave Suite 202, Lake Wales FL 33853
For more info call: 863-679 -2800 Website: www.melpercy.com

<u>The Mystic Moondragon</u>

Todd and Lisa Hammond

The first thing you notice upon entering this *"not so usual"* shop is the aroma of soaps, oils, lotions and potions that waft out of it as you step inside the door. These specialties are made-to-order and are custom-mixed according to your preference.

This gift shop carries other items that are as unusual as the name implies. Here, you will find authentic Mexican Sterling Silver and Peruvian Jewelry. Lisa is an accomplished photographer and has a collection of her works on display. Lisa specializes in nature photography.

The Mystic Moondragon now carries replicas of Medieval and Celtic swords. The collection includes replicas made famous by movies such as "The Lord of the Rings", the King Solomon Sword and King Arthur's Excalibur. While there, check out the selection of Japanese Samurai swords and daggers.
Many of The Mystic Moondragon's swords come with sheaths and wall plaques suitable for hanging your prized possession.

If you are downtown, step inside the Arcade to see Todd and his black cat, Mystic.

The Mystic Moondragon
229 E. Stuart Avenue Suite 10
Lake Wales FL
863-676-2004
Email: mystic_moondragon@msn.com

Salon Salon

Linda Bell Pineda

Linda is originally from Dryden, New York, but moved to Lake Wales in 1979. Linda has established herself as a prominent merchant in the downtown area for over 25 years.

For the first 7 years, Linda did business in the historic Grand Hotel. She then relocated into the Rhodesbilt Arcade Building where she stayed for 14 years. She has since purchased the building that now houses Salon Salon. Linda's business is located on Stuart Avenue, and the building is listed on the National Register of Historic Places.

Over the years, Linda has witnessed many changes to downtown Lake Wales. One of the newest and most dramatic transformations to the outside wall of Salon Salon is an original mural, 80-t long and 20-ft tall, painted by the artist James R. Hahn. Linda specifically requested Hahn for this project. The mural showcases lush, tropical gardens with Florida palms; and features a summer cottage that takes advantage of existing architectural details of the building.

If you are visiting downtown, stop by Salon Salon to see the mural. You can't miss it.

Salon Salon is located at 252 E. Stuart Avenue, in downtown Lake Wales. Linda invites you to stop in to say hello, or call her to book an appointment @ 863-676-2633.

Linda is a great stylist; you just may find your look, transformed, as well.

Stuart Avenue Café

Keith and Jacqui Johnson - owners

The Stuart Avenue Café is affectionately referred to as "a small place with big taste", but it really is so much more than that. Stuart Avenue Café is owned and operated by Keith and Jacqui Johnson from Liverpool, England. The restaurant offers a full menu, featuring both English and American fare. Food is served in a comfortable, relaxed atmosphere. A large selection of wine and beer, imported from all over the world, have turned Stuart Avenue Café into a popular, local watering hole. The central location of this International restaurant, has made it a designated "meeting place. Families, groups, clubs, and other organizations, now book the Café as their own, convenient rendezvous point for private parties and reunions.

The Café is located, street level, in the historic Gibson building, diagonally across from the Rhodesbilt Arcade. Look for the British flag in the front window, under the full length balcony that runs across the building's façade. Reserve your table for an authentic, English Sunday lunch. This traditional British repast includes: Roast Beef, Yorkshire Pudding, English Roast Potatoes and English Truffles, all served with your choice of wine or an English Ale. Call ahead, and Jacqui will prepare her famous English Scones for you to eat in, or take out. Ask Jacqui if she has any of her homemade Tangerine Marmalade. This mouth-watering spread tastes great on hot, buttered scones. For larger orders, groups, or parties, Jacqui and Keith will deliver your food *to* your home or office.

Stuart Avenue Café is located at 216 E Stuart Avenue.
For information or reservations, call 863-676-9000.
email - stuartavecafe@hotmail.com

Join Jacqui and Keith for dinner, you'll be glad you did.

Tres Jolie

French Pastry & Artisan Gift Shop
Harold & Jessica Bray

Tres Jolie was created by Jessica Bray, who shares her passion of French food, with her love of one-of-a-kind art treasures. The interior of the shop sparkles like a jewel box brimming with small antiques, ceramics, and French-milled soaps.

Tres Jolie is a local destination with the ambiance of a Parisian street café. This fabulously chic establishment is both a French pastry shop, and a gift gallery filled with vintage hats and purses, hand-crafted jewelry, objects d'art and collectibles.

Jessica studied at the prestigious Le Cordon Bleu Cooking School. She has won numerous awards for her baking skills. Assorted French pastries are made fresh daily and include: croissants, cheese cakes, breads, éclairs, tarts and jams.

As you browse this lovely gift shop, the aroma of fresh, French roasted coffee, cappuccino and espresso, fills the air and transports you to an authentic, French sidewalk café.
These delicacies are created and served, in Grand French tradition.

Tres Jolie is currently expanding into a larger Downtown venue and is slated to be a real show stopper. The new facility will include a private lounge, quietly tucked away and secluded from the main room. This cozy salon is reminiscent of an elegant French parlor, and can be reserved for private events. For more information, call Jessica @ 863-676-4142.

The Vanguard School

Dr. Cathy Wooley-Brown - President

The internationally recognized Vanguard School is located just three miles from historic downtown. For over 40 years, this accredited school has helped students with learning differences, such as ADD and dyslexia, discover their true potential.

Students are identified by their strengths, not weaknesses. Class sizes are small in keeping with the school's mission of providing support for the growth of each student. Their success rate is astounding. Over 95% of Vanguard's students go on to attend college. Attention to detail is apparent on this colorful campus. Beautifully remodeled dormitories are a home-away-from-home for students who come from all over the world to attend classes in sunny, Central Florida.

Varsity and Junior Varsity athletic programs teach students the value of competition through sportsmanship, teamwork, and school spirit. Prospective students are encouraged to visit the beautifully renovated campus. Arrange a meeting with the faculty and dormitory staff. Observe classes. Students are eager to share their academic experiences.

At Vanguard ... school spirit is contagious.

The Vanguard School
22000 Highway 27
Lake Wales, FL. 33859
Call the admissions office at 863-676-6091 to schedule an appointment, or visit online www.vanguardschool.org

Weaver & McClendon, PA

The law firm of Weaver & McClendon, PA has been a fixture in the downtown Lake Wales area for over thirty years.

Jim Weaver, a founding partner in the firm, is a graduate of the University of Southern Mississippi and the University of Georgia School of Law. Jim focuses his practice in the areas of estate planning, and real estate and business transactions.

Jay McClendon, a native of Lake Wales, is also a partner in the law firm. Jay graduated from Vanderbilt University and the University of Georgia School of Law. He practices primarily in the areas of commercial and real estate litigation, homeowners associations, construction law, and bankruptcy.

Jason Penrod, a graduate of Niagara University and Vanderbilt University Law School, has been an associate at the firm since 2004. Jason's primary focus is elder law. He also concentrates his efforts on Medicaid planning, probate, and Social Security disability.

Weaver & McClendon, PA is comprised of dedicated professionals who work in one of the city's restored, historic buildings on Park Avenue.

These professionals are proud to be part of our downtown community, and support the Main Street merchants with their participation in daily activities and special events.

Weaver & McClendon, PA is located at 240 East Park Avenue, Lake Wales, Florida.

Polk County

Facts & Fun Things to do

Polk County

Polk county is a nature's lovers paradise with it 36 parks and more than 250 different species of birds. You can bike or hike the many miles of nature trails. Polk County is a haven for many native creatures such as bobcats, alligators, deer, raccoons as well as indigenous and migratory birds.

Included below are just *some* of the area attractions:

Polk Outpost 27

This new, state-of-the-art visitor center, showcases all that Polk County has to offer. Watch an informative video in the high-definition theater to learn about the area's rich history and family attractions. Pick up brochures, visit interactive kiosks, and plan to have a good time. Make Outpost 27 your first stop. Located on Hwy 27 just south of Interstate 4.
Call 800-828-7655 for information.

Historic Bok Sanctuary

Located on the highest point in peninsular Florida, Bok Sanctuary features 128 acres of exquisitely landscaped gardens that encircle the park's spectacular 205-ft.bell tower. This impressive tower houses a 60-bell Carillon that rings out over the landscape, adding a cerebral experience to the tranquil sanctuary.

There are plenty of shady benches scattered among ancient, moss-covered oak trees, where you can relax and take in the breathtaking views of the surrounding citrus groves.

While there, visit historic Pinewood Estate, a beautiful and stylish home of Mediterranean Revival Architecture.

Guided tours allow you go from room to room to enjoy the splendor of the house and grounds. A special tour, not to be missed, is during the Holiday Season when the house is beautifully decorated for Christmas. Listen, and you will hear the bells of the Carillon, ring out in song, during an afternoon recital.

Lake Kissimmee State Park

This is the perfect place for nature lovers to step back in time to the Florida Wilderness of the 1800's. Walk the miles of nature trails, do some bird-watching, and see alligators in their natural habitat.

Be sure to visit the *Cow Camp,* located on the property.
See cows that are the actual descendents of the livestock of Florida's early Spanish settlers.

Talk to a real *"Florida Cracker"* to learn about cattle ranching in 1876. If you ask, he will demonstrate how to "crack a whip" and you will see how this name came to be used for these Florida cowboys.

You may ask this cattle rancher questions that are pertinent to the 1800's. But be prepared if you ask him modern-day questions... he will not have an answer for you. He will tell you, with a straight face, that he doesn't know what you are talking about! The year *is* 1876 ... after all.

Cypress Gardens Adventure Park

Cypress Gardens is Florida's first theme park.
Originally famous for its lush gardens and water-ski shows, this park has expanded and now features more than 40 rides, including 6 roller coasters.

In addition to the gracious, Southern Belles in hoop skirts that you still see strolling the park, Cypress Gardens Adventure Park offers impressive wildlife displays, a Bird Aviary and Butterfly Arboretum.

Check out the All-Star concerts, holiday events and daily shows. Bring your swimsuits for family fun at Splash Island Water Park. [Seasonal]

Florida Skydiving Center

If you are looking for a sky-high adrenaline rush; this is your jumping off point, literally. Here, you can parachute from a plane over Lake Wales.

Take a tandem jump and feel the wind in your hair as you fall 14,000 ft. at a speed of 120 mph. What a Rush!

Fantasy of Flight

The world's largest, private collection of vintage aircraft.
At Fantasy of Flight, see over 40 vintage aircraft, including a B-17 bomber.

A flight simulator will take you "up and away." Or rise above it all in a colorful, hot-air balloon. In season, reserve a bi-plane ride for a true, classic adventure you won't soon forget.

The Lake Wales Art Center

An old Spanish mission-style church, on Hwy 60, is now home to The Lake Wales Art Center. Enjoy special art exhibitions, musical performances and concerts.

The center provides tours, lectures and educational programs. Check out the annual, outdoor art show.

Lake Wales Museum and Cultural Center
(The Depot)

Downtown, in the historic district of Lake Wales, you will find an interesting museum and cultural center located in an old railroad station. The Depot, as it is affectionately named by the locals, features permanent exhibits from Lake Wales' rich history.

Ridge Art Association

Located in Winter Haven, in Polk County.
The art gallery is located within the Theatre Winter Haven Complex.
Exhibits, including annual juried art show.

Lake Wales Little Theatre

Restored, community theater located in Historic Downtown Lake Wales.

Theatre Winter Haven

Theatre Winter Haven has been called one of the best community theaters in America.

Spookhill

Spookhill remains somewhat of a mystery, and has fascinated visitors from around the world.

Cars parked at the bottom of Spookhill seem to defy gravity and roll uphill. Check it out. Its free, fun, and a little spooky.

Florida's Natural Growers
Grove House

Experience Florida's citrus industry up close. Grove House features exhibits on nutrition and horticulture. Sample some of the freshest orange juice in the world, and learn fascinating facts about Florida's official state fruit. Don't miss the video tour showing how orange juice is made.

Camp Mack's River Resort

Camp Mack's is a world-famous fishing resort on the Kissimmee River. Take a Airboat or Swamp Buggy ride across the water to see alligators, turtles, herons, egrets and osprey, in their natural setting.

Camp Mack's River Resort is located in Central Florida's Lake District which is named the "Largemouth Bass Capital of the World" because anglers catch so many of the fish here. . Other fish including bream, crappie and catfish abound in these waters, as well. There is also an RV Campground available for guests who really want to get close to nature.

Note- You can purchase a fishing license at any local bait shop or marina.

Lake Rosalie Park

From SR 60, east of lake Wales, turn North onto Tiger Lake Rd. Then West onto Rosalie Lake Rd.

Fishing, boat ramp and primitive camping are available in a beautiful, scenic Florida setting.

Lake Wales Ridge State Forest
Walk-in-Water Tract

Hike 20 miles on the Florida Trail. Birdwatchers should keep their eyes open for Florida scrub-jays. Bring binoculars to fully enjoys all the sights. Primitive camping is also available.

Lake Wales Ridge State Forest - Arbuckle Tract

Fish and canoe on four bodies of water. Look for playful otters on the banks of Lake Reedy. Hiking trails are marked by the Florida Trail Association.

It is recommended that you get a trail brochure before you hike. Great bird watching along trails. Bring your binoculars for an up-close look.

Tiger Creek Preserve

A 4,778-acre preserve is host to 15 of Florida's rarest species. Tiger Creek Preserve is located on the edge of Lake Wales' Ridge. Enjoy nature in an unspoiled setting.

Crooked Lake

This lake, one of the deepest in the area, features beautifully, clear water. Crooked Lake is especially good for bass and bluegill fishing. This blue lake is a fisherman's delight.

Winter Haven Chain of Lakes

Chain of 16 connected lakes. Great for fishing and boating activities. Family fun on the water.

Area Golf Courses

Lake Wales

Lake Ashton Golf Club
Lekarica Hills Golf Course
Mountain Lake Golf Course
Oakwood Golf Club

Winter Haven

Cypress Wood Golf & Country Club
Four Lakes Golf Club
Lake Bess Country Club
Lake Henry Golf Club
Lake Region Yacht & Country Club
Willowbrook Golf Course

Sports

Two Major League Baseball teams call the Lake District their *home-away-from-home:*

Cleveland Indians- Winter Haven - Chain of Lakes Park
Detroit Tigers - Lakeland - Joker Marchant Stadium

Single A Lakeland Tigers - play year round
Gulf Coast Indians - Minor League team - Chain of Lakes Park

Football

The Lakeland ThunderBolts - Indoor Football League
Orlando Predators - Arena Football League

Spring Training Games

Atlanta Braves @ Disney's Wide World of Sports - Baseball Stadium

Houston Astros @ Osceola County Stadium - Kissimmee
New York Yankees @ Legends Field - Tampa

Basketball

Orlando Magic - Orlando
Tampa Bay Storm - Arena Football
Tampa Bay Buccaneers - Raymond James Stadium

Hockey

Tampa Bay Lightning - @ St Pete Times Forum - St. Pete

The **Central Florida area** is known as the ***"Destination of Champions"*** because of the world-class staging environment and the close proximity of two major airports and major attractions.

Central Florida is nationally recognized as a leader in the sports field. The following organizations are all based in Central Florida.

- US Olympic Committee Governing Body
- LPGA Duramed Futures Golf Tour Headquarters
- Florida Youth Soccer Association Headquarters
- Independent Softball Association
- USA Water-Ski

Afterward

Cooking as an Art Form

The plate is a blank canvas.

With a desire to create, you can transform an empty plate into a mouthwatering, edible work of art.

Presentation is the visual appeal.

It is the contrast of pattern and color ... literally, the icing on the cake. With the right presentation, your dish will look as spectacular to your eye, as it is satisfying to your palate.

Garnishing is the finishing touch.

This is the stroke of highlight for your creativity. With objects extracted from nature such as an orange slice twist, a sprig of mint herb or something as simple as a colorful wedge of a vine ripe tomato, you can embellish your creation so that it becomes a true ... ***work of art.***

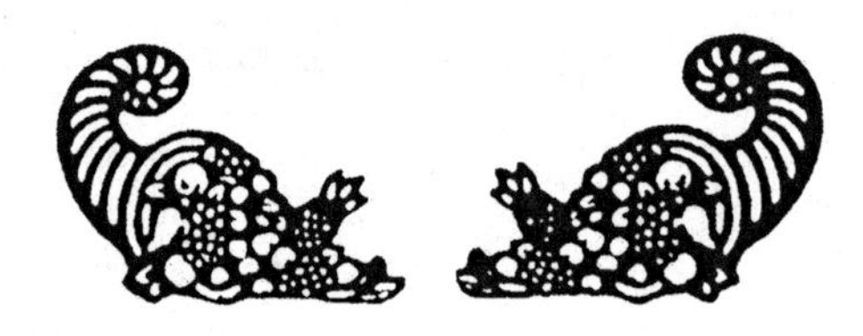

General Cooking Terms

Bake	To put food directly in a oven surrounded by heat. Food is set on a rack so heated air can circulate around the food.
Baste	To moisten foods during cooking, with water, pan drippings, sauces, and marinades, to add flavor or to keep foods from drying out during the cooking process.
Blanch	To pour boiling water over food. Used to loosen skin, or to remove or set color in foods.
Blend	To combine two or more ingredients until smooth.
Braise	To brown quickly in hot oil and then add a small amount of liquid and cook slowly in a tightly covered pot or pan. Braise on top of range or in the oven.

Broil	To cook or brown with direct heat. Place food on rack in oven directly under broiler unit to cook and brown food, turning as needed.
Dredge	To coat or sprinkle with flour or another fine substance.
Flake	To break lightly into small pieces. Example: Canned tuna is flaked to break up the larger pieces before adding to a recipe.
Fricassee	To cook by braising. It is a term usually applied to fowl.
Glaze	To coat with a thin sugar syrup that has been cooked to crack stage. Used to coat foods such as pies or breads.
Knead	To press and work dough with the palms of your hands, by turning and working a small amount of dough after each push. Use to work bread to distribute yeast and mix to proper consistency.
Marinade	To immerse a food, such as meat, in a sauce containing herbs, spices, or other seasonings. Marinating allows food to absorb flavors. Standing time for food to marinate can be as short as one hour, or as long as overnight.

Sauté — To quickly cook a food in oil or butter until done or tender. An example is to sauté onions in butter to brown and tenderize them in preparation of adding them to other ingredients in a recipe.

Simmer — To reduce heat after a food or sauce has cooked. Slow cooking a sauce such as a spaghetti or tomato sauce allows herbs/spices to blend and steep flavor into the mixture.

Slow Cook — To use an electric crockery utensil that cooks food at a low and safe temperature. Food can be placed in a slow cooker in the morning and cooked all day without maintaining the food or the cooker. Most slow cookers have two heat settings: Low and High.

- end of terms -

Substitutions

Don't have exactly the ingredients needed for your recipe? Substitute!

This list comes in handy at times when you need to change one ingredient for another either because you don't have the listed ingredient or you need to make a dietary substitution.

FOOD	**AMOUNT**	**SUBSTITUTE**
Buttermilk	1 cup	1 tablespoon lemon juice/or white vinegar plus milk equal to 1 cup.
Broth Beef/chicken	1 cup	1 bouillon cube/or 1 teaspoon granules in 1 cup water.
Cottage Cheese	1 cup	1 cup ricotta
Cornstarch	1 tbsp	1 tbsp flour
Whipping Cream	1 cup	4 ounce frozen Whipped Topping
Garlic	1 clove	1/8 tsp garlic powder
Herbs	1 tbsp fresh	1 tsp dried

Mustard	1 tbsp prepared	1 tsp dried
Onions	1 small	1 tbsp instant Minced/or ½ tsp onion powder
Sour Cream	1 cup	1 cup plain yogurt, ¾ cup buttermilk/or Evaporated milk + 1 tbsp lemon juice
Sugar	1 cup Light Brown	½ cup packed brown sugar + ½ cup Granulated sugar
Tomato Juice	1 cup	½ cup Tomato sauce + ½ cup water
Tomato Sauce	1 cup	½ cup tomato paste + ½ cup water
Yogurt	1 cup	1 cup buttermilk 1 cup milk + 1 tbsp lemon juice

Other substitutions include:

Cumin	-	substitute chili powder
Ginger	-	use allspice, cinnamon and nutmeg
Paprika	-	cayenne pepper (sparingly) cayenne is much hotter than paprika
Red Pepper	-	2 or 3 drops of hot sauce
Chili Powder	-	dash of hot sauce

Spice Blends

Barbeque Seasoning:
Zesty combination of spices with a husky, smoke flavor. Spices for barbeque blends include: Salt, sugar, hot red peppers, onions and hickory-smoke flavoring. Great used on meat before grilling or roasting.

Cajun Spice Seasoning:
Hot, spicy blend of garlic, onion and salt. This seasoning blend is typically used in Cajun cooking, and includes the *Cajun Trio* of black, white, and red pepper.

Herb Blends

Herbs de Provence:
Mélange commonly used in the South of France region includes: Basil, fennel, marjoram, lavender, sage, rosemary, savory and thyme. Great in pasta dishes, soups, salads and salad dressings.

Italian Seasonings:
Basil, oregano, rosemary, thyme, garlic and red pepper are the main herbs that are often included in Italian seasoning.

Jamaican Jerk Spices:
Lively Caribbean blend of sugar, salt, ginger, cloves, thyme cinnamon, onion and chili pepper. Gives an extra kick to fish, chicken, salad dressings and meat marinades.

Lemon Pepper:
Seasoning mix of salt, black pepper and grated lemon peel. Adds a slight lemon flavor to vegetables, poultry and soups.

Mexican Seasoning:
Hot and spicy blend includes chili peppers, cumin, oregano, garlic, and both sweet and red peppers.

French Terms

Fines Herbes - *pronounced [feenz erb]*
A delicate mix of parsley, chives, chervil and tarragon. This French blend is used to enhance gravy mixes and sauces. Fines Herbes imparts a robust flavor for soups, stuffing and casseroles.

Mire Poix - *pronounced [mihr-pwah]*
A mixture of diced onions, carrots and celery with herbs, sautéed in butter. Add to soups, stews and other entrees.

My Favorite Recipes

____ *page* __________

____ *page* __________

____ *page* __________

____ *page* __________

____ *page* __________

____ *page* __________

____ *page* __________

____ *page* __________

____ *page* __________

____ *page* __________

____ *page* __________

____ *page* __________

____ *page* __________

My Personal Notes

Order Forms

MAIN STREET FLAVORS
ORDER FORM
Fill out and send with a check, or fill out credit card information,
for $25 (per book), which covers a copy of the book, shipping & handling.
Florida residents please add additional $1.05 (per book) to your total for sales tax.

Name ____________________
Address ____________________
City ____________________
St __________ Zip __________

Quantity of books: __________ Check number: __________

Visa/MC info: Name on card: ____________________
Card number ________ ________ ________ ________ Exp date: ________

Mail to: "K Hahn Publishing" / 229 E Stuart Ave Suite 15 Lake Wales FL 33853

- -

MAIN STREET FLAVORS
ORDER FORM
Fill out and send with a check, or fill out credit card information,
for $25 (per book), which covers a copy of the book, shipping & handling.
Florida residents please add additional $1.05 (per book) to your total for sales tax.

Name ____________________
Address ____________________
City ____________________
St __________ Zip __________

Quantity of books: __________ Check number: __________

Visa/MC info: Name on card: ____________________
Card number ________ ________ ________ ________ Exp date: ________

Mail to: "K Hahn Publishing" / 229 E Stuart Ave Suite 15 Lake Wales FL 33853

Order online at www.mainstreetflavors.com

Printed in the United States
102747LV00002B/1-100/A

9 781432 717322